ADHD

A Complete Guide for Adults to Understand ADHD

(Impulse Control and Disorganization Through a Mind Process for a New Life)

Stephen Clark

Published By Chris David

Stephen Clark

All Rights Reserved

ADHD: A Complete Guide for Adults to Understand ADHD (Impulse Control and Disorganization Through a Mind Process for a New Life)

ISBN 978-1-77485-240-8

ISBN 978-1-77485-240-8

Legal & Disclaimer

The information contained in this book is not designed to replace or take the place of any form of medicine or professional medical advice. The information in this book has been provided for educational and entertainment purposes only.

The information contained in this book has been compiled from sources deemed reliable, and it is accurate to the best of the Author's knowledge; however, the Author cannot guarantee its accuracy and validity and cannot be held liable for any errors or omissions. Changes are periodically made to this book. You must consult your doctor or get professional medical advice before using any of the suggested remedies, techniques, or information in this book.

Table of Contents

Introduction

There are many problems with our children that can cause them to be classified as special children with special needs. Certain children may suffer from simple difficulties with learning or behavioral issues, food allergies and terminal illnesses, as well as developmental issues, panic attacks, and serious psychiatric disorders. Some of them may be able to catch up quickly or remain stuck.

A child with special needs is defined by the food they can't eat, things they are not allowed to do, experiences they are not able to take on and the things they are unable to accomplish. These disabilities can cause families to suffer huge pain and make these children appear to be an unimaginable tragedy.

There are parents who grieve and complain about the things their children are unable to accomplish. Some families are very happy when their children conquer obstacles and also know in the minds of their child's weaknesses will be followed by their advantages no regardless of the length of time it takes.In short, there are no two families who have children with special needs are alike. This is due to the fact that when one family could have an individual with a mentally ill child, another might have an infant who experiences anxiety attacks.

The problems encountered by these children can be classified as behavioral, medical, developmental and learning issues as well as mental health. There are also problems that are common to all children with special needs.

In a brief overview:

Medical problems

Include serious illnesses like cancer and muscular dystrophy; long-term diseases like diabetes and asthma. Also, there are congenital disorders such as dwarfism, cerebral palsy, food allergies. Children with these conditions will require lots of medical attention, most of which will be buried in the pockets.

Issues with behavior

Include children suffering from issues such as ADHD or Dysfunction of Sensorial integration or fetal alcohol spectrum disorder. These children won't respond to regular discipline, and require specialized methods that are appropriate for their particular type of problem. If the parents do not take this into consideration it will be difficult for the children to be easy to manage. The ability to think creatively and with flexibility is a requirement of parents.

Issues with development

This can be a huge blow to families because everything must be adjusted in order to ensure the child can be a part of the rest of the family. This includes intellectual disabilities, autism, Down syndrome. Children with these conditions aren't able to be at the normal schools, and parents must fervently defend their children's interests throughout the entire spectrum.

Leaning problems

This is especially true for children with dyslexia and central auditory processing. There will be challenges for them regardless of how gifted they may appear. They need a solution that is specifically tailored to meet their specific needs, so that their self-esteem is not damaged and their abilities are fully realized and any troublesome behavior that they might exhibit can be accommodated. Parents of children with these issues need to be persistent in order to be able to accept the child who is hesitant to learn and work together with schools their children attend.

Mental health concerns

This is especially true for children who suffer from anxiety or depression. These children may be sneaky on their parents and often suffer from attachment issues. A child with mental health issues can be feisty and has mood swings that are constant and is prone to having a variety of problems. Parents must seek assistance from a professional and to be able to take decisions , however challenging, and stick to them like the hospitalization process, therapy, etc.

Common problems

Children who have special needs need treatment, acceptance and support from all including their immediate family as well as routine and expectation. Also, it is important to think about the future because there is a chance that something will happen that can catch you out of your routine. Parents of these kids have to be more caring resilient, tough, and flexible than parents of normal children.

Chapter 1: Understanding Adhd

Someone with ADHD is unable to control their energy levels, which is why they are hyperactive all the time, anyplace. This is the reason ADHD children are often referred to as troublemakers or troublemakers in schools since they are unable to sit still for more than a few minutes. For some, this extra energy is accompanied by a plethora of talkative and annoying ways such as the use of words to insult a fellow student or irritating them with a gesture or poke.

Patients suffering from this condition struggle to concentrate and paying close attention. It is difficult to follow instructions for people with ADHD. ADHD is also characterized by impulsivity, which is, performing things without thinking about the implications.

The tasks at school and at home not always completed or never completed because they're either too boring or don't match with the brain's signals for moving around. While this might be normal for many children but it is especially problematic for kids with ADHD.

The brain is the most important part of it, ADHD is a neurodevelopmental disorder. This means that the development and growth of central nerves are affected. It affects areas within the brain, which deal with control, attention, cooperation, motivation and reward. In fact, the behavior patterns related to ADHD affect the capacity of an individual to perform in school and at home.

ADHD is among the most frequent mental health issue that affects children. As per the US National Institute of Mental Health that three to five percent of adolescents and children suffer from ADHD However, others believe that the number could be greater, at around 8 to 10%.This disorder can persist in adulthood for some.

Researchers believe ADHD is inherited. There is a chance of 25% that someone with ADHD will have a family member who suffers from the same problem.

For people who suffer with ADHD it is possible that they be struggling with time management , as well as at the work. Some sufferers are not organized and have lack self-esteem. It can be difficult for people with low self-esteem in setting goals, and to achieve the targets.

ADHD is classified into three kinds: inattention as well as hyperactivity and impulsiveness. The first kind of ADHD tend to be easily distracted, don't follow instructions or complete tasks that are given to them. they are not attentive and are prone to making mistakes. They tend to forget their plans during the day and have difficulty organizing their day-to-day tasks. It is normal for these types of ADHD people to be averse to or dislike sitting in a solitary position. They may be frequently snoring, or losing items easily.

Children who are diagnosed as hyperactive type typically fidget or squirm. They fidget and bounce around and move from one spot to the next. Additionally, children with this kind of disorder are unable to play quietly because they could be violent or susceptible to fighting. Along with being restless and agitation, they are also talking.

The people who suffer from impulsive ADHD have a hard time learning to be patient and wait their turn. They will always prefer to be first and be in control. It's not uncommon for them to give answers before they have finished the question. If your child is constantly interrupting your discussion during the course of the conversation and also when they are surrounded by classmates who recite the same thing, then they are suffering from hyperactive ADHD.

Chapter 2: Parenting a Child with Adhd

The raising of children with ADHD has its own unique challenges as they don't react effectively to the normal parenting techniques. A further issue is that parents may suffer from the same disorder , resulting in experiencing issues with consistency and organization. In this case parents too need to be trained to master the techniques.

Parents education and support groups are recommended to assist families to accept an ADHD diagnosis as well as to educate parents on ways to help the child to organize their space, manage the frustrations and devise strategies for solving problems. Education for parents is essential in educating parents on how to handle the child's worst behaviour with non-violent methods of discipline. It can also be beneficial to seek out individual or family counseling.

Understanding the basics of ADHD and establishing friendships with people who help you to care for your child can go a long way in helping you become a strong representative for your child. Take advantage of every opportunity for guidance and education, and lead your child towards the path to success.

Here are some strategies for parenting children with ADHD:

Limit your own behaviour.

Lucy Jo Palladino, Ph.D is a psychologist who is clinical and the author of Dreamers, Discoverers and Dynamos What to Do for the Kid Who is bright, bored, and having Problems at School.She states that the majority of parents are prone to worrying about their children and then rescuing them. Parents must realize how much they care for these kids as parents, the less they will be able to do for themselves. Parents' role is support their children, not get in the driving seat.

When working on work, Palladino says that it is acceptable for parents to inquire with their child whether they require one or another to finish the task. However, it can become complicated if the parent chooses to purchase a pencil and begin to tackle the assignment with their child.

If the parent's goal is to supervise the child as is doing their homework and homework, then the parent should include their own tasks, such as office work.

Allow your children to make educated decisions.

Children who suffer from ADHD tend to get lost in the flow of time and face a challenge in terms of being on top of their work. In general, it is said that children who suffer from ADHD appear disorganized in their attempts to accomplish anything they are assigned. This is the opinion of George Kapalka, Ph.D, an educator and psychologist in the field of clinical psychology and author of books about ADHD.

He states that in as much as this is the situation, your child has to develop self-control. One way that he suggests is giving your child plenty of opportunities to choose of how they should respond.

There is a method known as structured method where the kid is given two choices with the intention of leading them towards the direction that they desire. For instance parents could ask their kid, "Do you want to clean your room or rake the back yard?" or "It is almost dinner time and your home work is not yet done, do you want to start with English or Science?"

Remain calm.

The majority of experts advise parents of ADHD youngsters that it's crucial to be calm throughout the day. Kapalka claims that when the parent's behavior is out of control, the child's anger can shoot up the wall, so any interaction won't produce anything positive. Parents who are prone to becoming overly reactive must keep an eye on themselves.

Another thing to keep in mind is that fighting with your child isn't going to produce great outcomes. For instance, when you are working on homework, try not to make it seem like fighting because it's already challenging enough without the addition of an argument. Parents should be able to diffuse rather than engage in arguments that bring to a distraction that can slow the process.

According to Palladino the first thing parents need to do is to tell the child, "I know that this is not interesting for you." Then, follow up by a calm hug. This will reassure your child that you are understanding the child and can guide them towards the proper direction. Be careful not to use phrases such as "You're complaining about something that does not benefit you at all.'

Make sure you have a pressure-free structure

The structure of a system will differ according to the age group, for children who are young it is about stars, as for an older child, it's calendars and planners. For all children, the rules laid out in the structure should be logical and clear. This is especially true for the bedtime. The creation of a structure can help manage distraction and chaos. For instance the structure you create would include an established time for homework, along with rights to complete the task successfully. Parents may also collaborate with their child's teachers in designing this framework.

Palladino insists that pressure needs to be released of this system in order for excellent results to be realized. A structure free of pressure doesn't use threats or punishments , and doesn't have unreasonable deadlines, as they can result in drama, fear, and hostility.

Utilize appropriate consequences

According to Palladino the parents can begin with asking their children what the final outcome would be in the event that they violated the rules. She says this will prompt the child to make commitments that are their own.

Additionally parents must also create and constantly reward positive behavior through positive consequences, and rebuke the negative effects of bad behavior. Kapalka claims that this helps children understand that for any incident, there's an outcome.

Rules can be broken, Don't take it personally.

Palladino claims that it's an inherent part of the child's development to at times violate rules. If you do you should correct your child in the same way an officer would do in the event of a traffic violation and he won't take it personally with a groan or shout at you. Make sure to correct your child in a consistent, respectful and in a matter-of-fact way.

Your child isn't acting out intentionally

The majority of parents with children suffering from ADHD typically make unintentional mistakes in thinking that their children intend to be a nuisance.

But, Kapalka says that children are driven by goals and are hoping that the actions they take will eventually allow them to obtain what they want like receiving a reward or avoiding things like chores, or bedtime.

Do not turn off the active child

The majority of parents, as per Kapalka attempt to transform an enthusiastic and determined child into one who says yes to everything, without even blinking an eye, and does not challenge the authority of others. This is a huge error.

He also advises parents to recognize that there will be instances when children do not follow through with what they are instructed, or protest or respond. Parents should be aware of that children are frustrated and the best method to handle their anger is to let them be known but in a respectful manner.

Make sure your child is protected whenever the need arises.

There will be times when parents need to be advocates for their children due to an indication that the children are suffering from an impairment and cannot do certain things in the same way that normal children would. But when they do this, parents should be cautious not to cause their children to be incapable of learning some skills within them. For instance, although you may advocate for the use of talking children's books, you should inspire them to master the art of red by spending time with the child or asking a teacher to aid you. Your child should be aware that you are willing to fight for them, but you must also believe that they can be better.

One issue at one time

Kapalka states that problems need to be dealt with in a single step, so parents must be aware of what is the first position and then which is next. The ability to let go of certain problems while dealing with other issues will take the pressure off of your child's ability to help and the ground will not be taken care of.

Learn more about ADHD

It is very difficult to work with your child's ADHD when you're not knowledgeable about the condition. Find out more about ADHD and attention to ensure that you understand the reasons for certain things happening to your child's daily life and and how to manage them and more.

There's a lot to be done for children suffering from ADHD and their learning cannot be stopped. Parents, for instance, need to support their children in learning to deal with the changes that are happening in their daily lives the most positive way they can. They need be patient and must concentrate on their children's strengths , not of their failings. Parents must also appreciate their accomplishments because this will help them be grateful for the achievements that their children have come.

Chapter 3: Diagnostics of Adhd

Attention Deficit Hyperactivity Disorder (ADHD) is thought to be to be one of the most prevalent neurological disorders of children and youngsters in the school age nowadays. It is certainly the most controversial disorder too. It is controversial when compared to the conventional Western (allopathic) diagnoses as well as treatment. What I've seen throughout my life are many youngsters "drugged" in order to "do better" in school. The current trend of treating children with drugs and labels may have negative consequences that they'll have to endure throughout their lives.

Nowadays, there are many doctors, psychiatrists, and psychologists doubting whether a disorder like this exists. They do not recommend psycho-stimulating treatment for "disorder symptoms" but rather look for alternative treatments. Children who suffer from ADHD have troublesome behavior at home, and 82%

of them are believed to have academic issues. Estimates vary from 5 to 14% students in school suffer from ADHD. Children diagnosed with ADHD are typically prescribed psycho-stimulant medications, with what appears to be concerns about any adverse effects, whether long-term or short-term.

Of the five million kids today suffering from ADHD Over three million are taking Ritalin (methylphenidate) which is only a cursory diagnosis from a medical professional that the problem is. The medical profession also seems to be more focused on managing the behavior of students through drugs than trying to identify the causes of the condition. There are however several theories available today which can help address the nature and cause of symptoms associated with the condition without the use of potential harmful drugs.

Diagnostics of ADHD

These guidelines comprise: applying the DSM-IV criteria when symptoms are present in more than one environments, with the symptoms negatively affect the child's academic and social functioning for at minimum six months on a regular basis. An objective assessment should incorporate data from parents and the teachers at the school or other professionals. The evaluation of ADHD should be accompanied by an assessment of co-existing disorders such as issues with language or learning to be considered as a whole.

The AAP seems to be worried that too many doctors are willing to prescribe a child psycho-stimulation medication without having any assessment of the condition. They often only talk to parents or provide the child a brief in-office examination before prescribing Ritalin immediately in default, without considering alternatives.

It is the National Association of School Psychologists (NASP) in their publication provides specific requirements that children must meet to be identified as having ADHD. The criteria does not just include DSM-IV guidelines, but it also meets the federal requirements for assessing children who are eligible for services in the field of education in accordance with the Individuals with Disabilities Education Act (IDEA).

Thus, school psychologists often have the responsibility of reconciling confused or uneasy parents (who believe that something isn't the case regarding their child) as well as school personnel (who adhere to strict federal guidelines to assist students who have particular needs) and medical professionals (that is able to label children ADHD and prescribes medications without testing).

In reality, if you ask me whether I've ever seen this type of "correct" diagnosis for ADHD.. It's rare! ... rarely. The most common scenario is that parents take their child to their family doctor when they discover that something isn't "right", with the child not paying attention at school. The doctor will make an immediate diagnosis of ADHD and will write an outline to test an ADHD medication since it is so common nowadays, and it's not a huge surprise. The signs and symptoms to confirm the diagnosis at the moment, and with the huge amount of processed sugars and sugars in diets that we consume nowadays.

Chapter 4: What are the ADH

Symptoms and Signs?

A diagnosis for ADHD is based on the combination of evidence from the observation of behavior, behavioral history as well as medical examinations, and an assessment of psychological health conducted by a certified psychologist. The behavior studies should also be evaluated in multiple environments.The reasons for this are that when a person is highly active or impulsive in the school environment however, they exhibit normal behaviors at home, ADHD is not the cause, however, there may be other factors like bullying or other problems that result on the behaviors. An extensive neuropsychological examination is required to determine that the behavior isn't caused by other mental disorders or other disorders like an underlying learning disorder or a the disorder of language that could be believed to be ADHD.Other areas to be assessed are the environment at home. This can be evaluated by keeping the child away from parents in a quiet environment and asking questions that are appropriate for the child's age that they are at ease in answering. Children who have been neglected, abused or neglected tend to be inattention or irritable and may be depressed.They are likely to appear disinterested from activitiesand seem to be in a different world.This could be misdiagnosed as ADHD.

ADHD is believed to be caused by developing the frontal lobe area within the brain.While the frontal lobe in humans isn't fully developed until 20 years old early symptoms of ADHD can be observed when children are very small children.ADHD behavior is usually evident at about 4 years old. age.It is suggested, however, to make a diagnosis for ADHD is not to be made with children younger than 4 years old. old.Teachers typically are the first to recognize that the issue in an child.The reason is they have a direct comparison tool that they can use to compare themselves with others children.It is possible to recognize a problem when a child appears to be being different than peers of similar age and development.Teachers must be educated about how to spot the first signs of mental disorders in order to communicate the issues to parents.Some signs that teachers need to be looking for are children who need a large amount of time for tasks, making many impulsive mistakes, often interrupting the teacher, refusing to remain at a desk when directed to or a constant chatter or talking when they are told not to.Early recognition is crucial in ensuring that the right treatments in place so that the child will have a higher chance of getting the job done.

Instinctive or hyperactive behavior which are usually observed first. Examples include fidgeting, squirming or squirming, inability to stay still, anger towards peers (hitting or kicking, biting, etc.)) and excessive energy. physical or verbal outbursts and impatience, continuous talking and interrupting other people. These inattention-deficit behaviors are often evident when children start the school. The child could become easily distracted experience issues following instructions and forgetfulness, or struggle with work and seem to be unaware of what's happening around them.

Boys are usually identified with ADHD more frequently than girls. The primary reason is that girls suffer from the disorder differently.Children with close biological relationship with a parent who has ADHD tend to be more likely to be afflicted by ADHD themselves.

ADHD in teenagers can be more difficult as they move up to higher grades at school. Instead of being with the same teachers and students throughout the day, they are facing many teachers and diverse students.The additional schedules of various classrooms, extra homework and a more difficult curriculum can be difficult for ADHD suffers.If children aren't diagnosed with ADHD throughout their primary years, it can be harder to identify during the teens years.Teachers are now spending little time for each child and may not be able to be able to recognize the symptoms and symptoms.Parents should ensure they stay on top of the things they are teaching their kids and eye on same signs and symptoms as younger children.One of the major distinctions is that children who are older might be able to lose the hyperactivity aspect of ADHD and develop into the inattentive type.

Aspects and Signs of Hyperactivity or an impulsive ADHD

Trouble with fidgeting, squirming, or remaining in one spot, or waiting for his turn

Excessive running, climbing or being destructive

It's difficult to play quietly even when you're alone

Extreme impatience, longing for things now

It's always "on the go", all the time, as if they were an engine running at full speed within them

Talking too much, interrupting or blurting out responses

The Symptoms and Signs of Attention Deficit ADHD

Makes rash choices

Can easily be distracted

Doesn't have a problem adhering to or following directions

Doesn't appear to be listening when spoken directly to

Has trouble being organized

Avoids or is not a fan of doing things for a long time

It is very forgetful, constantly finding things.

Chapter 5: Effects Self-Help, and When to Get Help From Outside For Adult Adhd

If you're only beginning to discover that you suffer from adult ADHD it is likely that you've been through the years with the unrecognized issue. You may have been labelled "lazy" or "stupid" due to your lack of focus or inability to complete tasks, and you might have started to imagine yourself as a negative person too.

ADHD that isn't diagnosed and treated may cause issues throughout your life.

Health issues both mental and physical. The signs of ADHD may contribute to a range of health issues, such as excessive eating, addiction and anxiety, stress and tension, as well as low self-esteem. It is possible to get into trouble for not taking care of crucial health checks, not attending appointment with your doctor, not following the instructions of your doctor, and failing to take your essential medication.

Financial and professional issues. Adults who suffer from ADHD frequently face career challenges and experience a sense of not being able to achieve. It is possible that you have difficulty maintaining your job, adhering to company rules, meeting deadlines and sticking to your 9-to-5 schedule. Financial management can be a challenge: you might be struggling with bills that are not paid or paperwork lost as well as late fees and the burden of debt resulting from impulsive spending.

Troubles with relationships. The signs of ADHD can cause stress on your love, work and family relationships. It is possible that you are fed up with constant reminders from family members to clean up, pay attention or organize. Your closest friends however could be feeling angry and hurt by the perception of your "irresponsibility" or "insensitivity."

The broad-ranging consequences of ADHD can cause feelings of shame, anger, hopelessness as well as a losing confidence. It's possible to feel that you'll never manage your life. This is why being diagnosed with adult ADHD is a great source of hope and relief. It allows you to understand what you're dealing with in the very first instance, and know that you're not responsible for your situation. The problems you've faced are a sign of attention deficit disorder and are not due to a weakness in your own or character flaws.

If you're suffering from ADHD It's easy to get caught up in thinking that something is wrong in you. However, it's normal being different. ADHD isn't a metric of capability or intelligence. Certain things could be more difficult for you however, that doesn't mean you won't be able to find your niche and succeed. It's important to figure out your strengths and then capitalize on them.

It's useful to consider ADHD as a set of characteristics which are positive and negative, as is every other set of characteristics you could have. Alongside the impulsivity, and disordered thinking of ADHD as an example there is often a lot of energy, enthusiasm, and creativity in thinking outside the box, and a continuous flow of innovative ideas. Find out what you're great at and create your environment to help you develop the strengths you have.

Self-help for adults with ADHD

With a better awareness of the challenges that ADHD faces and the support of structured strategies you can implement real improvements in your life. A lot of people suffering from ADHD have discovered useful ways to deal with their symptoms, make use of their strengths and lead fulfilling and fulfilling lives. It isn't necessary to seek intervention from outside sources, at least not immediately. There's plenty that you could do in order to assist yourself and bring the symptoms in check.

Make sure you exercise and eat well. Regularly and vigorously, it helps to burn off energy and aggression in a healthy manner and also soothes and relaxes the body. Consume a range of nutritious foods and avoid sugary food in order to lessen mood fluctuations.

Make sure you get enough sleep. If you're exhausted and exhausted, it becomes even more difficult to concentrate, handle anxiety, be productive, and stay in control of your tasks. Make sure you get at least 7-8 hours of rest each evening.

Practice better time management. Make sure you have dates for all tasks, including seemingly insignificant tasks. Use alarms and timers to keep track of your progress. Pause at regular intervals. Do not pile up paperwork or delay by tackling each task when it is received. Prioritize tasks that are time-sensitive and write down each assignment message, request, or significant idea.

Develop your relationships. Plan activities with your people you know and be sure to keep your engagements. Be attentive in conversations Pay attention to what others are speaking , and try to not speak too fast yourself. Build relationships with people who are understanding and compassionate of the challenges you face with ADHD.

Make sure you have a comfortable working environment. Use lists frequently as well as color-coded reminders, notes-toself and routines, as well as documents. If possible, select tasks that are interesting and inspire you. Consider when and how you perform best, and implement these principles to your work environment the best way you can. It's a good idea to work with less inventive or organized individuals - a collaboration that is mutually beneficial.

When is it appropriate to seek out help for adults with ADHD

If the signs of ADHD continue to get into your daily life, despite efforts at self-help to deal with these symptoms, it's the time to seek out outside help. Adults who suffer from ADHD may benefit from a variety of therapies, including counseling for behavior, individual therapy as well as group counseling, self-help education assistance, and medications.

Treatment for adults suffering from ADHD, similar to treatment for children, must comprise a team of experts together with the person's relatives and their spouse.

Experts who have been specially trained in ADHD can assist you:

Control impulsive behaviors

Manage your time and budget

Stay organized and keep it that way

improve productivity at home as well as at increase productivity at work control anger and stress

More clearly communicate

Chapter 6: Physical Training To Control Adhd

ADHD is typically triggered and worsened by an imbalance in the levels of dopamine. In addition to regulating these levels by making changes to your diet and physical exercises like yoga, meditation and exercises to ease ADHD symptoms and gradually treat the disorder. This article will explain how these methods will benefit your child as well as how to help them to engage in them.

Physical Activity and Outdoor Playtime

Exercise can boost your mood, concentration and confidence through the increase in levels of hormones that improve mood such as serotonin and dopamine. Because these neurotransmitters are associated with improved endurance, confidence, and stamina A rise in their levels aids in reducing ADHD symptoms and helps your child to manage the disorder.

Additionally, for children who suffer from ADHD burning off some of the extra energy throughout the day could aid in bringing about an equilibrium in their hormone levels, and also help the child in to build good joints and muscle.

It is a good idea to encourage your children to participate in activities like running, walking or swimming, participating in an activity, etc.

Tai Chi

Numerous studies have shown that tai chi may help to reduce ADHD symptoms. Tai Chi is an Chinese martial art that is practiced for its health benefits, as well as to improve defense. According to the research team it was found that teens who suffered from ADHD and who practiced Tai Chi were less hyperactive and anxious. It also revealed that they did not think about daydreams as often. So, you can send your child in a Tai the chi class and be amazed at the difference.

Yoga

Yoga can be a great way to relieve anxiety, stress and negative thoughts, and helps to calm the mind , and increases confidence and self-confidence so that you are able to better manage your illness.

Additionally, a study released in 2013 revealed significant improvements in hyperactivity, anxiety, and social issues among boys with ADHD and who regularly practiced yoga.

Here are some yoga poses you can inspire your child to perform. It is recommended that you practice yoga with them to ensure they can see yoga as something interesting.

Child's Pose

The child's pose is an excellent yoga posture that can stretch hip and back muscles, and soothes the entire body. It can also help calm the mind, and offers immediate relief from the effects of hyperactivity.

To practice it, kneel on the floor directly or on your mat. Bend towards the front until the body is resting on your thighs, and your forehead rests upon the floor. Do this for two to three minutes or for 5 minutes if you could do it for more time. Repeating this every day calms down your hyperactivity and creates the feeling of equilibrium.

Chair Pose

The chair posture is ideal to boost confidence, posture and energy levels. It also helps improve concentration, which can aid a child in battling ADHD efficiently.

To try it out start by standing straight. Then gently lower your legs until they reach an angle that is similar to one you're at while sitting in a chair. Then, lower your hips and thighs in the amount that is comfortable and keep this posture between 20 and 60 minutes.

This twice a day boosts the energy levels of a child and also provides the child with the power and strength to better manage ADHD symptoms.

Alongside the exercises listed above to help treat ADHD it is also possible to create structure in your child's everyday life to control ADHD. Making sure that they have routines throughout the day that they can anticipate and build into routines can assist in managing the symptoms.

Chapter 7: What to Know The Child With Adhd or How To Manage and operate an Adhd Kid

The first step to owning and managing a child suffering from ADHD is to learn about ADHD and how it affects an particular child. Parents need to be experts in ADHD and not depend on the opinions of others regarding the child.

If parents trust their guts and trust their instincts, they are able to be impartial in their observations of the child's behavior as they know their child better than any other. A well-informed parent is confident in the their choices regarding problems the child is facing and are able to more effectively take part in the management process and track their child's progress.

Understanding the three main features of ADHD which include impulsiveness, inattention, and unregulated activities - permits parents to assess the child's behavior using an objective lens and determine realistic expectations.

It is not known absolutely the root cause of ADHD. The majority of evidence suggests it's a neurological, developmental brain disorder that affects at least one of the fundamental cognitive processes that are related in the capability to focus and maintain focus as well as to manage physical and cognitive impulsivity and to control verbal and motor activities.

Parents panic when they hear "brain disorder" and need to understand that having ADHD doesn't mean that the child is suffering from brain damage! Actually, ADHD once was called "minimal brain dysfunction." It's a good thing it was called "minimal" and thank goodness the name was modified to indicate more clearly that ADHD is a physiological. It is widely believed that an imbalance of neurotransmitters, dopamine and norepinephrine is a key reason for the root in the disorder.

ADHD is a blanket term to include subtypes of the disorder: the predominantly inattentive type - displayed by distractibility and problems of sustaining attention, disorganization, and forgetfulness; the predominantly hyperactive/impulsive type - displayed by activity and fidgeting, moving about at inappropriate times, unable to sit quietly when required, constant talking and blurting out; the combined inattention and hyperactive type and the not otherwise specified (NOS) type.

According to the American Psychiatric Association, ADHD is a disruptive-behavior disorder characterized by on-going inattention and/or hyperactivity-impulsivity occurring in several settings and more frequently and severely than is typical for individuals in the same stage of development. The behavior must have been in place for more than six months and begin at least seven years old.

DSM-IV Criteria to Diagnose Attention Deficit Hyperactivity disorder

According to DSM-IV the person who has Attention Deficit Hyperactivity Disorder should be diagnosed with either (1) either (2):

(1) (1) Six (or or) of the symptoms of inattention persist for at least six months in a manner that is unadaptive and incongruous with the developmental stage:

Inattention

(a) frequently isn't paying focus to the details or makes erroneous mistakes in work, schoolwork or other tasks.

(b) is often having difficulty paying attention to tasks or playing activities.

(c) frequently isn't able to hear when directly spoken to.

(d) frequently fails to adhere to instructions and is not able to complete chores, schoolwork or responsibilities at work (not because of a hostile attitude or inability to comprehend the instructions)

(e) frequently has trouble organizing activities and tasks.

(f) typically avoids, is not a fan of, or is not willing to engage in activities that require a constant mental effort (such such as homework or schoolwork)

(g) typically loses things that are essential to perform tasks or activities (e.g. toys and school assignments, pencils books, or even tools)

(h) is frequently distracted by stimuli from other areas.

(i) is frequently unintentionally forgetful during daily activities.

(2) Six (or more) of the following symptoms of hyperactivity-impulsivity have persisted for at least 6 months to a degree that is maladaptive and inconsistent with developmental level:

Hyperactivity

(a) typically fidgets with feet or hands or squirms in the seat

(b) typically leaves seats in the classroom or in other situations where remaining sitting is the norm.

(c) frequently runs around or climbs up when it is not appropriate (in adults or adolescents, it could be restricted to subjective emotions or restlessness)

(d) is often having difficulty playing or participating in leisure activities without interruption.

(e) is typically "on the go" or frequently acts as if "driven by a motor"

(f) typically talks in excess

(g) frequently blurts out answers prior to questions are completed.

(h) frequently has trouble waiting for turn

(i) typically interferes with or disrupts other people (e.g. interrupts or interferes in games or conversations)

Some hyperactive-impulsive or inattentive symptoms that caused impairment were present before age 7 years.

A few impairments from the symptoms can be seen in more than one place (e.g. at work or school as well as within the family).

There must be a clear indication of a clinically significant impairment to academic, social, or occupational performance.

The symptoms are not solely in the course of Pervasive Disorder, Developmental Disorder, Schizophrenia, or other Psychotic Disorder and aren't better explained by a different or different mental illness (e.g. mood Disorder, Anxiety Disorder, Disassociative Disorder or personality Disorder).

Attention Deficit Hyperactivity disorder, Combination Type: If both A1 and A2 criteria have been fulfilled for the past six months.

Attention Deficit Hyperactivity Disorder Predominantly Inattentive Type Criterion A1 satisfied however Criterion A2 hasn't been fulfilled for the last 6 months.

Attention Deficit Hyperactivity Disorder, Predominantly Hyperactive-Impulsive Type: if Criterion A2 is met but Criterion A1 is not met for the past 6 months.

Source: American Psychiatric Association: Diagnostic and Statistical Manual of Mental Disorders Fourth Edition. Washington, DC, American Psychiatric Association 1994.

Criteria for the Diagnostic Statistical Manual (DSM) defines the criteria for diagnosing ADHD symptoms, they must affect everyday activities. Some of the symptoms have to be present prior to the age of 7 symptoms that are documented in various settings, and be are present for longer than six months. It is important to note that the DSM cannot be used as a diagnostic tool that is used by educators or parents. The criteria outline begins with the description of the disorder to help diagnose it, however the child and disorder are more complex than a simple list.

It is commonly believed that Attention Deficit is that you are not paying attention In reality, children are attentive. However, their focus is on distracting, unimportant things, instead of the crucial and they are not paying attention when asked to do so by other people. They are able to and will concentrate on something of self focus and self-directedness, or, in the sense of doing what they would like to do, whenever they are motivated to.

Hyperactivity is often the most well-known characteristic of children in social and school situations , and it is the one that gets the most immediate reaction from adults. The term "hyperactivity" has a life of its own and causes people to wrongly believe that all children suffering from ADHD "bounce off the walls."

Children with ADHD have hyperactivity. Girls are less obvious by activities. Children who aren't hyperactive have difficulty maintaining attention and organization; they are also easily distracted; They are also generally quiet and quiet. They are less likely to have serious behavior problems, are more sluggish; and are more likely to be described as drowsy and slow-moving and are less likely to be criticized by their peers but more socially insecure.

Teachers would say to me "Your son is hyperactive and has a lot of other problems." They did not know that "other problems" were inattention and impulsivity. They also did not know about ADHD. So long as the child didn't wander around or disturb their class they wouldn't really care whether he was paying attention or not. It's true that hyperactivity may be only issue.

Through the years the child's lack of attention to small details, not finishing assignments, or not paying attention in class can affect the child's learning and progress. It is impossible to learn if he's not paying close attention.

The character of impulsivity is an unanswerable issue. A child who is unable to hold back his turn, to chase goals, delay the gratification as well as to be rewarded with the future rewards is viewed as morally deficient and socially unfit.

Parents frequently ask "All kindergartners fidget, don't sit still, have difficulty waiting turns, etc., so what makes my child ADHD?" Teachers tend to think that they must be in a room with a lot of hyperactive kids. What differentiates the child suffering from attention deficit hyperactivity disorder from the rest of his peers and siblings is the extent, frequency and the age-appropriateness of the behavior. Furthermore, the symptoms persist over time and are present in many circumstances.

In the last couple of decades, the awareness of ADHD has substantially been increasing. This is because parents like me accept the responsibility of learning about the disorder, and work with medical and educational professionals to understand the impact of ADHD on their child and offer appropriate treatment.

Due to the increased awareness that ADHD is a growing issue, there's an abundance of information on ADHD. There are often newspaper and magazine articles as well as news stories on TV and radio and there are many books about the subject and support groups, and there's the internet. There is a lot of conflicting information regarding ADHD as well as unsubstantiated treatments. All of this information could overwhelm parents who are informed that their child is suffering from ADHD.

Being aware of the condition is vital in managing the ADHD lifestyle as well as managing expectations from adults and also the behavior of your child. The more parents are aware how to manage the disorder, the better they will be in discerning information and making appropriate treatment decisions for their child.

Chapter 8: Adhd Diet, The Foundation Of Healing Of Adhd

Dr. Natasha Campbell-McBride has provided us with the insight that there's more than appears to be the case in the context of why the number of individuals who suffer from mental illnesses is rising. In the United States, one in 150 children are diagnosed with this disorder while genetics are the primary explanation but it's not the sole reason explain the rise in the number of healthy people and those suffering from developmental issues. Doctor. McBride says that genetic changes take longer to manifest and therefore, it's not the sole cause.

Dr. Campbell-McBride has examined hundreds of autism patients as well as psychiatric illnesses and learning disabilities. She discovered that nearly all of them indicated that patients had digestive issues. Her research has revealed that Dr. Campbell-McBride identified that the bowel flora is unhealthy and a poor digestion, as well as toxic the chemicals in foods that are not digested which adversely affect brain's chemical. The correlation is known as Gut as well as Psychology Syndrome or as Dr. McBride calls it as GAPS.

There is a question that arises: what is the reason a new child be diagnosed with problems like ADHD as well as autism and also get ill-distributed food? It is due to an issue that is inherited and family-basedin the absence of adequate nutrition from their parents and grandparents, every generation has less healthy children.

What is GAPS?

Children who are diagnosed with mental disorders actually are physically sick. They are susceptible to allergies to pollen, animals dust, chemicals, and of course food. They also have other issues like asthma, eczema, digestive issues and infections. Adults and children with ADHD or depression as well as autism cannot digest and absorb the nutrients in their diets properly which is why they suffer from nutritional deficits. Due to this they are not able to function in a normal society.

Adults and children with digestive problems fall under the Gut and Psychology Syndrome, or GAP Syndrome. If they are diagnosed with mental disorders, they may not receive the appropriate treatment due to the fact that most doctors do not know the causes of these conditions and how to treat them effectively.

In GAP syndrome GAP Syndrome, kids and those with mental health issues generally exhibit these traits:

They suffer from digestive disorders or have had an ongoing digestive disorder at one time in their lives

They are usually allergic and Eczema is a frequent ailment found in babies, adults and infants.

They are also malnourished appearing pale and sallow

ALL DISEASES ARE ENTRIERED in the GI

Over two millennia back, Hippocrates once said that every disease begins within the gut. This claim could not be more apparent in the modern world in the present. Nearly every disease starts in the gut. When considering degenerative illnesses, regardless of how unrelated they may appear it is always beneficial to examine the digestive system.

If you take a look at infants with colic, you will see that the condition present in them is the result of an imbalance in the gut flora. This should be a wake-up call in parents to take urgent steps to normalize their baby's gut flora, because if this isn't addressed, it could result in serious problems later on.

When it comes to GAPS children, the overproduction of gas results in flatulence and bloating, which is common among teens, children and adults. They also experience constipation and diarrhea occasionally.

MALABSORPTION and OSTEOPOROSIS

Another issue GAPS adults and children have to deal with is the issue of mal-absorption. Their digestive systems do not take in food properly and as a result they suffer from numerous nutritional deficiencies.

The brain as well as the immune system are affected as it is unable to function properly without proper nutrition. Deficiencies in nutrition cause many issues including arthritis and osteoporosis.

If adults and children go to the GAPS nutrition program, initially they gain pounds before they begin to grow. In the case of a child lacking nutrients will be replaced by the body before the child gets bigger. Similar is the case for adult.

THE GUT FLORA

To put it into simple terms the gut flora can be described as an assortment of yeasts, bacteria virus, worms, viruses and single-cell structures that reside within the digestive tract of our body. In the adult state the microbes could weigh between two and three kilograms.

The interaction between bacteria and the human body can be described as a symbiotic relationship. They are essential for our daily lives in a way that when our digestive tracts were to be sterilized, we'd most likely be dead. The microbes that live in them are beneficial to us which is why they're often referred to as probiotic microbes.

The benefits of probiotic microbes

They create anti-biotics for the body

They produce antiviral and antifungal substances needed by the body to defend itself against pathogenic microbes in food and drinks

Probiotic microbes also shield your body against carcinogens as well as toxic substances through neutralizing them

The benefits of a healthy gut flora

A healthy gut flora forms an enormous protection for your body from anything harmful. If you eat a lot of fish, you'll be protected to a greater level from mercury poisoning.

Even if probiotic microbes are unable to eliminate these toxic substances inside the body, they is able to excrete them out of the body.

Gut flora that is healthy produces many kinds of enzymes vital to our body's health all over the world that break down carbohydrates, proteins, and fats. They also release vital vitamins and minerals into the body.

It also aids in the production of nutritious compounds for the body, including B vitamins such as B1 and B2, B3 as well as B6, B12 biotin and folic acid. The gut flora also makes vitamin K2.

GUT FLORA AND IMMUNE SYSTEM

The immune system within our body is dependent on the health of the gut flora. There are two components of our immune system, which comprise the Th1 immunity and Th2 immunity. Immunizations go together to establish the optimal balance of protection to your entire body. Th1 is the one responsible for normal reactions to surroundings. For example, if take in millions of particles of pollen, it is likely that you won't be affected or experience any allergic reactions since Th1 immunity handles the environmental factors. Th1 is present in all areas within your body, which come into close contact with the outside world like your the skin, your tears your saliva eyelids mucous secretion, and even the sexual organs.

The immunization system is broken down as the gut's flora gets weak. The next the line of defense would be Th2 which is the one responsible for allergic reactions, but it begins to become hyperactive as it attempts to compensate for the weak Th1 defense. In this situation it makes the person more sensitive to the entire environment from pollen to fur mix with different food sources.

In the flora of a healthy man is a mixture of around 500 species of pathogens that are bad and fungi which coexist with beneficial bacteria. If the beneficial bacteria are dominant in the gut, there's absolutely no damage to your body. If the bad bacteria are dominant that is, both children and adults are more susceptible to illness and illnesses.

When GUT BACTERIA goes wrong

When the gut becomes sour it is the time that kids and adults experience dysbiosis in the gut. The most prevalent type of microbe found in the gut at present can be found in the Candida species that is a huge group of yeast that has 200 species. When beneficial microbes exist within the gut, candida and the other yeasts that cause harm, remain in single-cell form and are not harmful in the system of immune defense or body.

However, the negative effect occurs in the event that your body doesn't have enough beneficial bacteria in your digestive tract, and this is when yeasts get stuck on mucous membranes , and then multiply and cause havoc to the normal bodily functions. There are a variety of yeasts, including Candida. exist within our digestive system, however with the beneficial bacteria in the system, everything within the body is functioning normally.

Healthy individuals have a good amount of sulfur and clostridia inside their digestive tracts and the amounts are controlled by the beneficial bacteria.

For autistic children for instance the sulfur content in the body is severely inadequate because sulfate-reducing bacteria eat the sulfur and, in turn, the body is over-using sulfur in order to handle the apex of toxic substances.

If examining a person suffering from mental illness when examining a patient with mental disorders, Dr. McBride examines the neurotransmitters which are the substances that are found in the brain, such as dopamine and serotonin. These chemicals are regenerated through the liver after they've finished their work within the brain and body. The process is dependent on sulfur and if your body is not able to produce it, the job can't be completed. If the body isn't able to make these chemicals in the brain then it is filled with debris from brain's neurotransmitters that have been damaged. Although these neurotransmitters are able to interact with neuron cells in our brains, the function is not 100% effective and can cause neurological and mental symptoms.

It is the same with those who suffer from mental illness, there may be virus infections in these people. For instance, Andrew Wakefield found measles virus in autistic patients. Another patient also had herpes virus.

The bottom line is that as long your gut is full by beneficial microbes, there's no way that pathogenic bacteria can infect your gut.

Nature has a decent way to fight bad bacteria. It fights it by introducing good bacteria. One way to ensure that your body is doing this naturally, it is best to first and foremost build an environment that is healthy, with good microbes and yeast.

A BRAIN DRUG THAT IS HARMFUL

What occurs when harmful bacteria invade in the digestive tract? The answer is that it turns the digestive tract into a source of toxic substances. The bad microbes that reside in the digestive tract consume the food items brought with it. They then transform it into hundreds toxins instead hundreds of nutrients. Then these toxins are released into the bloodstream and across the body up towards the brain.

In essence those with ADHD or autistic, or adults suffering from ADHD or depression - these toxic substances are already present within their brains. Sensory information can be affected by the fact that the brain a child is filled with toxins making information difficult to process.

Due to this the children and adults suffering from ADHD as well as autism and other mental disorders don't do well in the social world frequently behave in strange ways and are unable to follow simple guidelines.

GUT FLORA HERITAGE

So , how do we affect our gut flora in such a young age? As you consider it, how can babies have a gut flora which is damaged? As we know, were born with an unclean digestive system and sterile bodies. As the baby is going through their birth, the first intake of bacteria comes from the food they eat in the birth canal and then it becomes their gut flora. Anything that is present in the birth canal of the mother is absorbed into the vagina of the mother, and becomes the baby's gut flora.

Prior to the introduction of contraceptives, including antibiotics, women generally had normal vaginal flora that was healthy and was passed on onto their offspring. However, with the years of antibiotic use, this alters the gut flora of women, so everything that is found in the bowels of women's reside in her vagina and then get transmitted to her infants.

A mom with gut dysbiosis may pass the disorder on to her baby and, in turn, the baby develops a faulty gut flora. This can affect the immune system of the baby. Establishing a healthy gut flora during the baby's beginning months of their lives is essential to ensure an adequate maturation of the immune system. when this isn't happening in the initial few days, the baby's immune system will be affected. This can set children up to suffer from a variety of health issues like asthma and allergies, atopic reactions and many other problems.

A child who is less toxic is stronger and will have a stronger structure and will be less susceptible. Additionally, based on the genetic makeup of the child and other environmental influences the child may have distinct symptoms. Some are diagnosed as having autism, while others will be with ADHD as well as some who suffer from mood swings, others with obsessive tendencies and others with depression.

STOPPERING COMPROMISED GUT FLOWER

Although mental disorders like Autism and ADHD are severe, they are treatable by the right treatment. The earlier a child is treated, the better the outcomes. Expect a 60 to 70 % of full recovery when the child is properly diagnosed at the age of three.

What kind of treatment do the GAPS system consider?

It is first and foremost intended to address the digestion problem which the majority of people be suffering from whether they are children or adults. Any mental or psychological disorder is, fundamentally the digestive disorder. It could be anything such as bipolar, schizophrenia or obsessive-compulsive disorder, drug addiction or depression. A physician trained in this GAPS system will first examine your digestive system.

NUTRIENTS

The GAPS method, there are two diets: the Introduction Diet and the Full GAPS Diet. The diets are implemented in phases and is the best choice for children as well as adults to begin to adjust to the lifestyle changes it demands. Dr. Campbell-McBride suggests that you follow the Introduction Diet for patients who have severe digestive issues as well as extreme food sensitivities. This is also known as the Full GAPS Diet would better fit those suffering from constipation or moderate food sensitivities.

The Introduction Diet

Introduction Diet Introduction Diet is divided into six stages. It takes between 3 and six months to finish each phase each stage lasting a week or less. For every person, it's a unique scenario. Some people may need longer to adjust.

It is a Introduction Diet is designed by Dr. Campbell-McBride to help patients who have severe digestive issues such as chronic diarrhea IBS gastritis, Crohn's as well as Ulcerative Colitis as well as patients suffering from extreme neurological conditions such as schizophrenia, autism depression, bipolar disorder, and schizophrenia.

Depending on how severe the neurological issues of a patient are depending on their neurological condition, some patients might be able to complete this Intro Diet a lot quicker than others. The most important thing is to be aware of your body and watch your body's reactions.

STAGE 1

Meat Stock

Well-cooked soups

Boiled Meat

A teaspoonful of fermented vegetable juice

The Ginger Tea is flavored with honey.

Stage 2. (Continue Step 1 Foods)

Organic Egg Yolks Raw Pastured from the Farm Added to Soup

Soft Boiled Eggs with Soup

Stews and Casseroles and Stews

Enhance Fermented Veggie Juice

Fermented Fish

Homemade Ghee

Stage 3. (Continue Stage 1 and 2)

Mashed Ripe Avocado in Soup

Nut Butter Pancakes

Scrambled Eggs with cooked vegetables and avocado

Cooked onions that are well-seasoned

Homemade Fermented Veggies

STAGE 4 (Continue Stages 1, 2 and 3)

Roasted, baked, and grilled Meats

Olive Oil

Fresh Made Veggie Juice

GAPS Bread

Stage 5. (Continue Stage 1 2, 3 and 4)

Cooked Applesauce

Raw Vegetables, Introduced Slowly

A small amount of fresh fruit juice as well as vegetable juice

Stage 6. (Continue Stage 1 2 3, 4 & 5)

Cooked Applesauce

Honey production has increased

GAPS Baked Goods

Begin each day with a cup or two of warm water at room temperature with the slice of lemon, and a commercial-grade probiotic. Wait at least 30 mins before eating. Baths for detox should be used at least one to three times per each day. A GAPS diet should include protein and animal fats as well as fermented vegetables, bones broths and meat stock.

The benefits of fermented foods

The increased amount of enzymes helps people to absorb nutrients, thus reducing the need for vitamins or supplements.

Probiotics from fermented foods can aid in restoring the gut and assist in digestion and immunization

The lactic acid produced in the process of fermentation destroys E. E. coli, making it much easier to eat raw vegetables.

The process of fermentation increases the nutritional value by enlarging certain nutrients

Examples of fermented food items like Sauerkraut Kimchi, Miso, Sourdough & Pickles

Bones and Meat Broth are beneficial for health. Broth

When the bone is simmering it releases powerful minerals like gelatin, collagen and magnesium. and potassium. Consuming these nutrients is beneficial for our health

It heals leaky gut, eases inflammation of the intestinal tract.

Reduces inflammation and fights flu and colds

Reduces joint pain and encourages healthy bones, tendons, ligaments

Calms the mind and encourages sleep

Aids in the detoxification of the liver

Benefits of a diet high in protein

Helps to Improve Muscle Mass by building strong muscles and tendons

-Helps you manage your weight. The consumption of protein triggers an internal process known as thermogenesis. This demands the body to use more energy to digest food.

Protein is an essential ingredient to balance neurotransmitters in the brain. It also synthesizes brain chemicals like dopamine and serotonin which helps to soothe nerves and keeps us optimistic.

Protein improves cognitive function. When amino acids have been introduced to the body brain function and motor skills are improved

Chapter 9: A Study in the Science

Behind Adhd

ADHD is not a new phenomenon; it has been documented in written form and recorded as a remedy for two centuries. ADHD is a perpetual illness that can be present various levels of severity, and every once in some time, it is not related to others. There are three main symptoms: the inability to concentrate, the inability to control movement and inhibitive behaviour that can lead to an impulsive behavior. In any event, difficulty with directing emotions is usually an issue. It is important to note that symptoms of ADHD vary from day to day, and hour to an hour, despite the fact that many children may display these symptoms. It is the intensity of the presentation that is the issue, not being able to direct them, and the degree of debilitationthat results in a decision.

What exactly is ADHD?

ADHD is a condition that affects children and adolescents. (ADHD) can affect children as well as high school students may progress to adulthood. ADHD is one of the most frequently studied mental disorder among children. The children who suffer from ADHD could be hyperactive and unable to manage their driving force. On the other hand , they may experience difficulties in focusing. These activities can interfere with the school schedule and family life.

It's more prevalent for young men than girls. The boys are about three times more likely than females to to have it, but it's unclear as to the reason. It's usually seen in the beginning of school in the beginning of a child's life, when they begin having issues with concentration.

Adults suffering from ADHD may have difficulty managing time, focusing in setting goals, and working. They could also be struggling with self-esteem, connections and habits.

Children with ADHD are impulsive or are overly active, and have difficulty focusing. They may comprehend what is expected from them but have trouble concluding their tasks due to the fact that they are unable to sit still, remain focused or pay attention to small details.

Naturally, everyone (especially youngsters) behave in this manner at times, particularly when they're stressed or excited. The difference with ADHD is that symptoms occur over a longer extended period of time and occur in various environments. They can affect a child's ability to be social, scholastically and even at home.

The good news is that with proper treatment, children with ADHD can learn how to live with and deal with their signs.

ADHD as well as Executive Functions (EF)

Recent research has shown us that children and adults who suffer from ADHD often have issues in the realms that are a part of the executive function (EF). The executive function is the process that allows us to organize ahead, analyze the past, initiate with and complete a task, and manage our time. The ability to be executive-functional allows us to recognize the problem, find solutions and compose ourselves, regulate our thoughts and behaviour manage our thinking levels, and resist distractions.

Working memory, which is a crucial element of executive functioning is a skill that allows us to store information in the cerebrum , and use it at the same time. Working memory directly affects comprehension of reading, written expression math abilities, and the ability to concentrate and resist distraction. Students suffering from ADHD are also able to time they process information that are coming in and out at a slower pace. The children who are lacking in these areas are frequently mistakenly portrayed as being unmotivated, disobedient and uninterested.

Types of ADHD

In the case of ADHD No one treatment or treatment can be completely matched. Everyone is unique. Scientists and experts have identified three kinds. Each one has distinct symptoms, and the medicines are based on those symptoms.

The three kinds of ADHD are

1.Inattentive Type

A patient with this sort must have no less than six of these nine symptoms, and not very many of the symptoms of hyperactive-impulsive sort:

Paying no attention to the aspect of interest

Making careless mistakes

Not paying attention and continuing in a given task

Do not pay attention to someone's talk

Not being able to follow the direction or follow the guidelines

Refraining from activities that require exertion and effort

Working or being occupied

The inability to concentrate

It is a loss of items that are needed to complete work.

2.Hyperactive-Impulsive Type

To be able to show this kind of behavior one must possess at least six of the nine signs, and not too numerous of the signs of unobservant type:

Fidgeting

Squirming

Sitting for a long time and getting up often

Moving or running at inconvenient time

Are you having trouble playing quietly?

Talking too much

Speaking out of turn, or screaming

Hindering

Sometimes "on the go" as although "driven by an engine".

3.Combined Type

This is the most frequent kind of ADHD. People with it have symptoms of both inattentive and hyperactive-impulsive types.

Affects of ADHD

ADHD is among the well-known disorder of mental health in adolescence. People all over the globe have documented the incidence of ADHD for children in the school age in the range of five percent and 12percent. This suggests that there is no less than one to three children in each class suffering from ADHD. The greater number of young males than girls are examined at a ratio of 3:1. However as young women tend to be less likely to display an outward display of hyperactivity and impulsivity and the same amount of women as men is examined in the adult years We realize that we do not recognize many girls who suffer from ADHD as they enter their adolescence. Females suffering from ADHD are as afflicted in areas of thought and social and academic issues as men. Eighty percent of children who were assessed as children continue to meet the requirements for determination, and among those children over sixty percent have reported that they had suffering from the symptoms until they reach adulthood.

Chapter 10: Things to Beware Of When You're afflicted with Adhd

Most medical experts agree that changing your diet will not be able alter any of the ADHD symptoms. The majority of these researchers do not suffer from ADHD. They may be right, and diet modifications don't affect symptoms of ADHD signs directly. However, research suggests the change in your eating habits may help with the variables that impact the severity the severity ADHD symptoms.

Stay Away From Caffeine

There are many reasons to eliminate caffeine from your diet if you suffer from ADHD and. Caffeine is a response to every ADHD medication that contains stimulants. Stimulant-based ADHD medications comprise Adderall, Ridelin, etc. These medications stimulate your system. If you mix them with caffeine, then the effects are "supercharged". In the beginning I committed this mistake when I was taking Adderall. My heart rate jumped from 170 to 180, and stayed there. The highest safe heart rate at my age the 186. My heart is in a risky state that is always.

Anxiety is also exacerbated by caffeine. Caffeine can cause people to feel anxious and jittery. Stress is among the most frequent symptoms of ADHD. Caffeine can trigger the anxiety symptoms of ADHD and make them more severe. Why would someone who suffers from anxiety would want to consume medication that can make anxiety more severe?

Eat Protein

A diet that is rich in protein has numerous benefits which can aid in ADHD. These should include lean protein like lean steak fish, chicken, and lean pork. ADHD symptoms result from certain brain regions producing more compounds than others. Proteins aid our brains neurotransmitters produce more substances. This assists in easing the problem that occurs in the chemical.

The body also makes use of protein to regulate blood sugar. Blood sugar drops can cause us to have trouble managing our mood, becoming angry, and suffer from headaches. A high blood sugar level can cause us to feel nervous and have a high level of energy, struggle to pay attention, and so on. These two issues are similar to many of ADHD symptoms. If we keep our blood sugar levels on an even level, we reduce the severity of our ADHD symptoms.

Eat Balanced Foods

All things must be handled in moderate amounts. A balanced diet is beneficial in controlling blood sugarand body fat and all the body systems function better. Our diets should contain complex carbs, vegetables, fruits and proteins. Many parents of adults suffering from ADHD as well as children with ADHD have observed their symptoms decrease when they eat eating a balanced diet.

Take nutritional supplements to treat deficiencies

Nowadays, everyone has life full of activity. Even our kids go to school, after-school events such as plays, group recitals and more. Try to control their food intake as adults also must manage ever-growing workloads, spending time with their families, and bringing students to and from their school activities. It is nearly impossible to include all vital fruits and vegetables in our diets.

Supplements for nutrition make it easy to receive the needed nutrients. A daily multivitamin provides 100percent of your daily requirements of a variety of vitamins and minerals. It is an excellent place to begin. Fish oil has been shown to alleviate ADHD symptoms. Look at your person diet. What are the foods you're not getting enough of? Find a multivitamin which could provide you with those nutrients.

Eliminate food items one at a time

It's easy to identify the cause of a food's impact on the severity of your ADHD symptoms. Begin by identifying food items that may be contributing to symptoms of ADHD symptoms. Like the ones above, possible triggers could be caffeine or sugar. Other colors could be yellowish, red as well as MSGs colorants for food. Select one item such as caffeine and eliminate all caffeine from the diet over a few weeks. The initial few days may be needed to remove the caffeine removed from the system. If you notice that your ADHD symptoms improve, remove that food from your diet. Repeat this process for other sugar or non-sugar foods to determine which ones are helping you.

Make sure you are prepared

ADHD research has grown many times over the last 20-30 years. Researchers are constantly learning more concerning our ADHD symptoms as well as their causes and ways to reduce the impact they have on our personal lives. Research conducted by private researchers keeps you up to current on the latest developments. This isn't as hard the task it may seem. There are many websites, websites that are social network that is dedicated to ADHD.

Nearly every aspect of our lives can be a source of. Our stress levels can raise. The body may be able to lack vital minerals and vitamins. All our body systems endure including our brains. Our ADHD symptoms may increase or diminish. Eliminating things like sugar, caffeine, as well as the red or yellowish food coloring can have positive effects for our well-being. Like The Dr. Pelsser found, they may even help to eliminate symptoms completely. Utilize an elimination technique to determine the foods that cause symptoms. In the event of any health issues such as diabetes, or any other medical condition, consult your physician prior to making any significant modifications.

The US alone, 9 percent of children are diagnosed as having Attention Deficit

Hyperactivity Disorder (ADHD). The majority of symptoms of ADHD are evident at the age of in the toddler stage and becomes more evident when the child reaches seven. The condition can persist for the child as the time he reaches adulthood. So, even adults could be affected. Teenagers and adults who suffer from ADHD typically have issues with inattention, hyperactivity and impulsivity. This can lead to the school, home and work, as well as play and weddings, to problems or difficulties.

Different treatments are being developed to treat the disease or at least lessen the discomfort caused through its symptoms even although the cause of ADHD remains a mystery. Some of the ADHD treatments include treatment, special drugs, as well as alternative medications or natural remedies. If the person consumes a lot of junk food there is no way to treat the problem, then none of these methods are effective, then they're not working. Since specific types of ADHD diets can increase the effectiveness of treatment for the disorder, diet is crucial.

The right diet for ADHD can boost the performance for the mind. This is why it could be beneficial for the sufferer regardless of whether they are an adult or a kid to adhere to an ADHD diet plan. Diets as they are generally understood by us restrict the consumption of certain food items, and this applies to people suffering from AHD. Why not extend the same diet to everyone in the family so that your child with a condition will not feel as if he's not getting the benefits. Actually, the diets recommended for those suffering from Attention Deficit Disorders are the same type of diet programs to that are recommended by athletes to help athletes perform better.

Below are some foods ADHD patients must stay clear of from eating, or taking in massive quantities.

Dairy products, especially cow's milk. Allergies are thought to be a contributing to the development of ADHD for both children and adults. According to the American Pediatric Association has reported it as a percentage that is approximately children are susceptible to dairy products like cow's milk. Refraining from dairy products, even for a short time could help reduce the risk of symptoms.

Caffeinated beverages. People with hyperactivity should avoid drinking caffeinated beverages like caffeine and other energy drinks. This is because caffeine-based products contain stimulants that might not be beneficial for ADHD sufferers.

Junk food. Junk food items are loaded with carbs and sugar. Junk foods are believed to contain properties that may prevent the mind from functioning more efficiently.

Sugar. Although no studies have confirmed that sugar actually is a factor in the onset of ADHD in children It is thought that children's behavior could be affected by excessive levels of sugar. A diet that is low in sugar could help to reduce the symptoms.

Fish. There are numerous benefits to eating fish. However, the inclusion of fish part of the daily diet of ADHD sufferers may not be advised at all. This is due to the fact that fish nowadays may contain high levels of mercury that isn't healthy or safe. Fish from deep oceans are an not an exceptional case. They are fantastic brain food (for anyone).

Foods that contain additives and coloring. Some are trying to connect the potential of food coloring and additives as a cause of ADHD.

There are a variety of foods that may be linked to the development of ADHD. There are numerous kinds of foods that will help to reduce the incidence of symptoms. Whatever the reason to ADHD for your kid or adult, the most effective solution is to offer the diet recommended for ADHD sufferers that can to improve brain functioning. By doing this, symptoms can be lessened.

Foods to avoid when treating ADHD The Foods You Should Avoid For ADHD Myth Or Reality?

A special dinner was prepared in the kitchen of Jamie Oliver the British food expert during last year's G20 summit for the world's leaders around the globe. Jamie Oliver is extremely proud of the fact that he was able to obtain $1million in funding from the British government to help improve the school meal. Take pizza chips, sausages and chips and in with salads, fruits and vegetables, as well as lean meats. What are the best food items that can help you avoid ADHD ? Certain foods are safer to avoid since they've been proven to be linked to disorders of behavior. Both the UK as well as the European Parliaments have passed legislation in this direction.

What is the most harmful foods to make sure that children don't start jumping off walls and don't be hyperactive? It isn't possible to select the right foods to help prevent ADHD but you can greatly reduce the effect. A majority of colourings and additives are not recommended. The colourings often referred to as"Dirty Six" are currently banned in the United Kingdom and Europe since research shows that other issues with behaviour and unacceptable conduct can be caused among children.

In regards to sugar, Jamie Oliver is certainly convinced that the amount of sugar needs to be drastically reduced in other junk fooditems, cereals and snacks. These are just a few of the foods that can be avoided for those with ADHD or an ADHD child. The author is even proposing the taxation of sugar! I'm sure obesity and diabetes will decline, though I'm not sure about ADHD. Studies have shown that sugar does not cause the level of restlessness or stimulates fidgeting. In the present, he's working with a well-known grocery chain in Britain teaching families how to prepare a healthy, delicious and balanced meal for $7.

That's how you can eat that help to prevent ADHD or at the very least limit the harmful consequences of processed foods. Numerous studies have shown that ADHD children are deficient in a variety of vital minerals and vitamins crucial for brain development. They can keep the mind functioning at its best. The reason they didn't have the essential elements is because they eat a poor diet. There are certainly many parents who aren't certain that they have certain foods to avoid for those with an ADHD child. If Jamie Oliver can do it for British families, then so can the Americans!

In addition to diet and what food items to avoid in the first place, there are plenty of other aspects that parents should be conscious of when trying to deal with ADHD. One of them is ADHD behavior therapy, which has saved many families from ruin. The other is to be able to read to ADHD natural solutions in lieu of ADHD

medications that can cause more issues
than they resolve!

Chapter 11: The Reasons

The jury is still debating about the precise cause or root causes of ADHD however, there appear to be some common themes that are surfacing strongly.If you're the parents of an child that has ADHD and has a history of it, it could be very difficult to blame yourself for the unruly behavior your child might exhibit due to this condition.One factor that can't be blamed for the cause is parenting mistakes, or the inability to discipline the child.So let's look at ways to eliminate the unhelpful notion right away.

What exactly is it?

It was thought the diet as a major contributing factor, but it has been questioned recently.Rather it's due to chemical imbalances or disorders in the brain.In children, some or all of these symptoms are present:

*Restlessness, not being able to be still

*Lack of concentration

*Forgetfulness

*Running about or climbing on objects without any awareness of risk

*Screaming in class, unable to keep their mouths shut and interrupts other students

*Seems like they're not really paying attention

*Talkative

Obviously, these symptoms are bad enough for a child.Their schoolwork suffers and their ability to make friendships with their peers and so they do not get a chance to become socialized.Inexperienced professionals may not fully understand the disorder and so the child receives inappropriate discipline.

If left untreated, it could cause more serious issues throughout the teens and adulthood.Teenagers who suffer from ADHD could be in troubles at school, as well as with police.The typical complaint of teens that their parents doesn't understand him may be the case in their case.They could turn to illegal substances, and then develop addictions. And obviously their academic results could be lower due to the lack of focus or inability to think things through to the finish.

As the person suffering from the condition grows to be an adult, issues may get worse and cause anxiety as a result of the issues that the condition can bring along it.There are a variety of symptoms , including:

Depression is the feeling of not being able to handle the situation

*Anxiety : worrying about whether or not you will be in a position to finish or complete something

*Relationship issues

*Moodiness

*Substance abuse may lead to addiction

Lack of concentration in reading or performing tasks at work

*Quickly vent anger and frustration

* Acting according to impulse

Self-confidence issues So many failures in the past

*Acting in impuls

No feeling of danger

*Can't stop talking

The Reasons

If we've identified what is not able to cause ADHD What causes it?

Genetics

There is evidence - with a 50% chance this disorder is passed on between parents via it's genes.It is also possible that if a child is affected, there's a 30 percent possibility that their sibling suffers the same.

Pregnancy Problems

If woman smokes or drinks during pregnancy, it could affect the development of the baby's brain.

Food ingredients

There seems to be a weak link between food additives and ADHD, but the FDA says that this link is tenuous at best and additives are not harmful to children.Nevertheless, it is likely that additives and food colorings will affect a small number of children.It is becoming increasingly common to find how harmful additives or substitutes can be.Why take a chance when you can prepare natural food yourself and know exactly what went into it?This can be done as a family and encourage the joy of cooking in your child.

Food allergy

The consensus among doctors is that food is only little or no role in ADHD.Nevertheless it can't be completely eliminated as the cause of some cases due to the fact that every person's genetic and physical constitution is unique.A significant proportion of children are sensitive to a variety of foods and this may trigger various symptoms ranging from mild to severity. One of these is ADHD.Fortunately there are many children who become immune to the allergic reaction as time passes, whereas some suffer from the allergic reaction and make ADHD manifestations worse.Food allergic reactions can be identified by a simple blood test, however this could be expensive and unlikely to be readily available even if the symptoms aren't serious or causing physical symptoms like breath loss or swelling, as well as rashes.Some typical food allergies include wheat in bread or cookie dough, dairy items such as eggs and milk, and unfortunately chocolate as well as fish and shellfish.It is possible to determine whether any of these food items can trigger an allergic reaction by removing them from your diet one by one to check if symptoms improve but you should consult your physician before making any changes.

In the following chapter, we will discuss traditional treatments, i.e., drugs and the risk it is in the event of any.By picking this book you've probably decided to seek out alternatives to treating ADHD however is this really useful or necessary?

Chapter 12: Setbacks to Adhd and Monitoring Your Progression

This chapter you'll discover:

ADHD Setbacks

Staying on Track

ADHD Setbacks

The chance of having a setback or slip ups in your development can occur to anyone at any time. In reality, the majority of people experience more intense symptoms of ADHD at times. The aim is not to let the minor setbacks take the worst of you. Keep in mind that every step back can be a chance to improve your performance.

I like to always provide an example of learning to ride a bicycle as a child. In the beginning, you'd fall and feel unsteady however, if you got back up and kept trying at it, eventually, you'll discover how to keep your in balance and avoid those mistakes that seemed to be so difficult initially. The process of developing new emotional and social skills is a huge process. It's not easy to deal with things that seem strange and alien, however it's the way you learn to deal with those difficulties and overcome the obstacles that will define your personality moving forward.

There are a variety of reasons why a setback can happen. Stresses from physical and emotional are among the most common causes for individuals' ADHD symptoms to recur. If you're stressed out it is important to use the strategies you've learned in therapy and implement them into your everyday life. There's nothing that isn't a challenge to overcome. Maintaining a positive outlook can benefit you in the near future.

As you get further into your therapy and are beginning to move towards the goals you've set yourself, you should realize that the problems you're dealing with currently are just a glimpse on your radar screen.

Many of these issues will not be thought of in a week, day or even a month from now. If you observe a rise in back-slashes on a regular schedule, make sure you follow the guidelines below to avoid a serious flare-up of your symptoms.

Find the warning signs and signs. One example is the moment you lose focus faster and more frequently and becoming more forgetful on a regular basis, feeling stressed more frequently or feeling as if the world around you is beginning to spiral beyond control.

You might want to work on improving your social and emotional abilities. Examine all the skills you've been learning through therapy (e.g. social skills training and learning to think before speaking and speaking).Are currently using the new abilities regularly as much as you could be? If not, you should consider incorporating these skills more frequently into your daily routine. Make sure to incorporate into your routine to make it automatic to you.

Maintain your mind positive. A positive outlook can benefit you in the end. Being able to see the positive in a difficult situation will enable you to overcome even the worst of times. Be aware that setbacks don't mean failures.

A support system is an additional important aspect. It's crucial to have someone to talk to and have a meaningful discussion. It doesn't have to be a lengthy session that involves pouring your heart out. It's about finding someone you can talk to and share all of your goals with and what's going on to you at this moment. Things will appear more significant in your mind. When you hear the issues being discussed it can provide you with a fresh perspective.

Aiden's Story

Aiden is suffering from a serious form of ADHD. The diagnosis was made at a young age because he displayed a variety of signs, and struggled with them quite a bit. His parents attempted to try therapies, however it was not enough. After they had come to this realisation, they quickly agreed to the doctor's advice and started him on medication.

The following one year Aiden was through a amount of highs and lows. Initially, he responded extremely well to the new medication regimen and therapy. But, in the next few months the doctor needed to start adjusting the dosage. In the following months after that, when it did not work and the patients switched to other medications. One month after that, they switched and began taking antidepressants.

At this point Aiden's mood and mood was constantly changing. At times, he would appear normal and comfortable but the next day, it would be like that he was spinning and out of control. The schoolwork was a constant nightmare and he struggled to relate to kids of similar to his older.

In all of it, Aiden always stayed upbeat. Even when he was at his lowest, Aiden would always put his best face on and make the most of the day with smile. Aiden's parents had instilled into him from a young age that staying positive could enable him to make the best of any difficult situation that was outside that of their control. Aiden believed that and it helped help him through the dark times , when they were trying to figure out a solution that was consistent.

In the end, the doctors have hit on the appropriate medication and dosage levels , and Aiden's symptoms have drastically diminished. The struggle with ADHD symptoms is an everyday aspect of his life, but he's confident that no matter how bad it gets that he has the stamina and mental toughness to conquer it.

Be Keeping Your Improvement

It's crucial to remember all the progress you've made in the time you've been in treatment. When you achieve the goal, it's best do yourself the favor of giving yourself a reward and make sure you take the time to appreciate these moments. Rewarding yourself with positive words is an effective way to keep you inspired to keep doing your best and applying the new abilities you've acquired. Maintaining your gains from treatment will require you to keep improving the social aspects of your life, adhere to your medication and treatment regimen, and keep educating yourself about new ways to overcome any obstacle that your ADHD puts in your way.

I've always been a huge lover of keeping a diary and logging the progress. I think it's a great tool to use both for creativity as well as in order to reflect on the accomplishments you've made in the course of the course of time. I convinced my niece and nephew to do this when they were diagnosed with cancer, and they've discovered it helps give them a sense of purpose on times when things get tough. A journal gives them to revisit and reflect through their own eyes all the good things that been accomplished, as well as the improvements they've achieved.

Julian's Story

Julian was diagnosed only after he had gotten was out of college. Julian had always been different from his classmates and familymembers, but he refused to admit that there could be an issue. In his place, he'd create excuses and try to justify his actions.

The girlfriend of his once laid down with him and said she believed it might be time to seek professional assistance. Julian ignored it and it wasn't until a few months after that his girlfriend ended their relationship and he reacted with anger at work, resulting in himself fired that he began to think it was possible that she was right. Julian studied his symptoms online and realized he could be suffering from ADHD.

Julian discovered that he was suffering from ADHD and immediately started treatment. It took a while and lots of therapy, but ultimately Julian was able to bring his ADHD under control at last, for the very first time in his life that he was able to feel like an ordinary person. In the following months, Julian had the occasional incident, and even failed to get off the medication. After he was aware that he must be vigilant about his health He pushed himself into the right place and has a routine in place to keep him in top shape. Julian finds himself in a a healthy relationships and doesn't let his physical symptoms determine the course the course of his existence.

Chapter 13: What are the Signs of Adhd?

There are three types of ADHD which include: hyperactive-impulsive, inattentive and mixed type Each type has its own distinct characteristics and symptoms.

Inattention

They are are struggling to concentrate on their tasks, which is why they are easily distracted. They tend to make mistakes in their work. They are also often distracted and are prone to losing personal items like wallets, notebooks, pens and even phones.

The type of person also exhibits symptoms of hearing loss particularly when they are engaged in something else that is interesting to them. They generally do not like or prefer jobs that require mental energy. They're not well-organized and are known as messy.

Hyperactive-Impulsive

On the other hand, Hyperactive-impulsive types are those that are usually playful, children who have this type of ADHD seem to be excessively energetic on their activities.

They also talk so much which makes their mouths extremely difficult to closed. In class, they're those who are always bursting out their answers before the class closes. It's very difficult for them to stay at a desk and be patiently waiting to be called upon. These types of people are perpetually "on the go" and always require something to focus their focus on.

All Together

The third kind, known as the Combined The Combined popular. It is also regarded as the most difficult to deal with because it exhibits all the symptoms of the previous two.

It is vital for everyone, particularly parents of children suffering from ADHD to bear in mind that those with this condition aren't necessarily bad. They just behave according to the rules their mind is imposing. The condition isn't completely eliminated, but it can be controlled if the proper focus is given.

In the last few years of research, the right medication and the use of behavioral therapy has been proven to be effective in treating this condition. Each child's needs are unique So make sure your child's needs are assessed by a trusted professional to ensure the most effective results from treatment.

Chapter 14: Adhd or Add Adults

Life is an exercise in balance for every adult. However, if notice that you are always delayed, distracted, chaotic or forgetful, and become overwhelmed by obligations, then it is possible that you have ADHD or ADD. Attention Deficit Disorder doesn't just affect children , but adults as well. There are many apprehensive symptoms of this disorder that could affect your relationships, life and professional career. However, there is help that is available at any time All you have to do is step towards your right direction. get some more about the condition. Once you have a grasp of the difficulties and obscure challenges you have to face, can you begin to tackle it.

To be diagnosed as having the disorder the adult must exhibit ADHD symptoms that started in childhood and continue through adulthood. Certain scales of rating are utilized in the hands of Health

Professionals to determine whether or whether an adult suffers from ADHD. The Health Professionals will also examine the person's behavior throughout childhood or school and speak to any person who is closely related to that person, such as siblings, parents or spouses, as well as friends. The patient will also be required undergo physical examination and a range of psychological tests. For some people, this diagnosis of ADD/ADHD could be a source of relief due to the fact that they could be suffering from the disorder from childhood and had a lot of negative perceptions of themselves. Once the issue is recognized, the appropriate kind of treatment can aid in overcoming it.

Knowing ADHD or ADD for adults

It is a popular belief of ADD/ADHD as a disease that affects children. This isn't the case. If you've had a diagnosis of ADD/ADHD as you were a young person it is likely you carried at least a few of those signs to adulthood. Even if you not diagnosed with ADD/ADHD when you were an infant, it doesn't necessarily mean you won't be in any way affected.

It was not common in the past, when attention deficit disorder would be ignored. There were a few people who knew of the existence of ADD/ADHD. In the absence of recognizing the condition that the child suffered of, the person was to be branded someone who was a dreamer, slacker or simply a bad student. You may have believed that these issues would disappear with old age, rather than experiencing more difficulties when the demands on your time increased. The more tasks you have to accomplish the more difficult it becomes to maintain your attention. It is difficult to balance your work and raising a family and managing your household is a challenge that can overwhelm your mind. . This is a challenge for everyone but, if you're suffering from ADHD or ADD, everything would appear impossible to manage.

The good thing is that no matter the way you feel the issue can be conquered. With an appropriate amount assistance along with education and a bit of imagination, the signs of ADD/ADHD can be cured.

MYTHS AND FACTS

Myth:

This is simply an absence of willpower. The people with the disorder can concentrate effectively on subjects they enjoy, and they are able to concentrate if they wish to.

FACT:

It could appear as if it's caused by determination and control. It's actually not. It's primarily something that happens to the brain's management system.

Myth:

Everyone is affected by the signs of ADD/ADHD, and anyone with sufficient skills can overcome these challenges.

FACT:

ADHD/ADD is a disorder that it affects all people of abilities. There is no distinction for it.

Myth:

If you didn't have ADD/ADHD as an infant, you won't be able to have it later on as an adult.

FACT:

A lot of adults suffer from ADD/ADHD, and it could be that it has not been recognized. It is possible that if you had been diagnosed with ADD/ADHD when you were when you were a kid, you could have carried some of those signs into adulthood, too.

SIGNS AND SYMPTOMS

The symptoms that children show for ADD/ADHD differ than those displayed by adults. The symptoms can vary from one person to the next. The best thing to do is identify the areas that are problematic for you and then develop strategies to address them.

The most common symptoms and signs are the following:

Trouble concentrating

Adults who suffer from ADD/ADHD are typically struggle with focusing and staying focused. Their focus span is extremely short. As an example, you may become bored very quickly, or cannot focus on just one thing for long. These are among the most commonly reported symptoms that are often overlooked since they aren't visible as disruptive. They aren't as bothersome as the other symptoms of ADD/ADHD such as the impulsivity and hyperactivity, but they are just as problematic. Inattention manifests in the following ways:

- Attention span is not great.

- Inability to complete basic tasks

- Poor listening skills

Hyper focus

A lot of people don't know that there are two impacts of ADD/ADHD in adults, and their tendency to be focused on tasks that simulate and reward. This phenomenon is known as hyperfocus.

This is in reality an effective coping mechanism when you look carefully for distraction, it's a method of focusing on the noise. It is so powerful that someone struggling with this may become too absorbed in one thing that they are completely unaware of everything that is happening around their. For instance, you may become so immersed in an episode on TV and reading your book you forget about time and completely forget the things you're supposed to be doing. This can be a benefit when properly channeled and focused on the right issues. However, if it's not managed properly, it can cause problems in relationships and life.

Disorganisation

It is an ongoing battle for any adult, however for someone who is struggling with ADD/ADHD, life might appear chaotic and uncontrollable. Being organized and on in control of everything may appear to be an overwhelming task. It can become very difficult as managing time becomes very challenging. The most common signs of this are:

- Deteriorating organizational skills

- Procrastination

- Chronic lateness

Inability to keep track of time

Impulsivity

You may have trouble controlling your actions and your comments and reactions. You could be inclined to act and act without thinking about the consequences. It is possible to struggle to control your the impulses you feel if:

Unable to hear an audio conversation

- Poor Self - Control

- Relapses to certain behaviors

Emotional Troubles

Common symptoms of emotional distress in adults with ADHD/ADD include: they are having a difficult time controlling their emotions and emotions:

Motivational issues

Always under stress

- Extremely confused and confused.

Very sensitive to criticism.

Hyperactivity

Many people suffering with ADHD or ADD, the signs of hyperactivity diminish and are less noticeable. Children's hyperactivity differs from hyperactivity among adults. It is possible to appear extremely active and constantly in motion as if you're controlled by some force. Some of the symptoms that can be attributed to the condition are:

- Extremely very agitated

- Unrestful

Always willing to take risks

Very fidgety

There is a common misconception that you have to be hyperactive to be diagnosed with ADHD or ADD. The signs differ based on the individual and their age.

Affects on ADHD or ADD

It is possible that you have found out that you suffer from adult ADHD or ADD. You're likely to have struggled through the years and didn't realize the issue was affecting you. You may have been criticized by people who wrote you off or described yourself as lazy or foolish perhaps. It is possible that you have thought of yourself in that way. It's not true. It's the fact. The best way to beat it is to learn more about it.

Mental and physical health issues

The signs of ADD/ADHD may be a cause of many problems such as addiction to food, compulsive eating anxiety and stress, chronic tension and stress and low self-esteem. Due to the numbness associated with this condition, you could get into trouble if you don't attend regular health checks, or ignore medical guidelines, etc.

Financial and work-related difficulties

Adults who suffer from ADD/ADHD typically have career issues and an overwhelming sense of being under-achieved. It is possible that you have difficulty following the strict rules of your schedule, working hours at work and deadlines

Relationship issues

The signs of ADD/ADHD may cause stress to the relationships that exist within your daily life personal and professional."

The negative effects of ADD/ADHD are vast and can result in shame, sadness, depression as well as loss of confidence, even anger. It is possible that you are plagued by the fear that you'll never achieve your goals. So dear reader, fret not. The problem can be solved by a little help from an ADD/ADHD specialist and your family members and, most importantly, some effort from you. The next chapter will provide detail how this could be accomplished. Read the final section to learn more about self-help methods that do not require medication.

Chapter 15: Medication and Marketing

Do we have to assume that the medication industries conduct research, market and sell ADHD medications due to the fact that they are passionate about children and would like to provide the highest for them? They want their children to do well in life? I'm not sure about this. ADHD is a hugely profitable business. According to what I've read and witnessed in life, it's all focused on money. If ADHD were not so lucrative, it wouldn't be as well-known, and less kids would suffer from it.

The history of the world reveals that ADHD wasn't always profitable. There was an era where children were diagnosed with real learning problems caused by various types of "minimal brain damage." These cases weren't as large, and they did not attract the attention of large pharmaceutical companies, in order to develop the number of brand names that we see today.

Healthy children were enticed into the sport through aggressive campaigns. The lists of symptoms were developed and promoted in imaginative Ads. Commercials featuring children who were distracted were shown. Research articles began to explain the issue of attention. Then, suddenly becoming tired and not paying enough attention was deemed an illness, and the diagnostic criteria grew. Parents with a skewed view began becoming concerned. The diagnosis spread around the world.

Children are among the victimized. Teachers and parents too are victimized for failing to determine what the true root of the problem is. Some psychologists and doctors have fallen victim to this ADHD trap.

In his book "Rich Dad Poor Dad," (2011) Robert Kiyosaki warns people against falling for ads: "A drug company runs ads on television in February, showing people getting the flu. The number of colds increases and so do the sales of cold medicines." Kiyosaki clearly exemplifies the reasons ADHD is so popular in the last couple of decades. Actually, ADHD is a profitable business since pharmaceutical companies were successful in their efforts to market their medications. It's not due to an epidemic, it's just clever marketing.

Films are based on the same model. A movie is advertisement in disguise. It's focused on the product. Once the movie is made, a plethora of products will be available on the market. If we're not cautious all that appeals to our eyes could be a way to brainwash us. Experts have this in mind which is why an advertisement on TV for 30 seconds in Super Bowl week in 2015 cost an estimated $4.5 million . (Kissanne 2015).

Some people are naive enough to purchase amazing products advertised on television at midnight. This is an obvious example of what human beings are known to behave.

Pharmaceutical companies aren't doing anything illegal, however the marketing of certain medications, like the ones used to treat ADHD is so inconspicuous that we do not even realize what's really going on. Another illustration of how marketing works can be seen in the film The Lorax which, I believe, veers away from the actual way of thinking and acting as the Dr. Seuss.

The film makes us laugh in our faces and we can't comprehend the humor. Two experts in marketing are selling empty bottle which are only filled with air. O'Hare is the millionaire of Thneedville states, "You gotta be kidding me. Are you sure that people are dumb enough to purchase such a thing?" One of them tells O'Hare: "Our research shows that the moment you put something in the plastic bottle and people buy it, they will as well. And that if we construct an entirely new facility to manufacture those plastic bottles, quality of air will only improve which will lead people want to breathe in to breathe in even more air and increase sales, but where? In the sky!"

Naturally, O'Hare did not disagree. He was not concerned about air quality, nor about the child who went swimming and is now glowing like neon. He only wanted to earn money. This is what some businesses do. In the beginning, they'll generate a need before the field is ready for harvest.

It's not difficult to gather evidence of the amount of cash drug companies spend on marketing (Statista 2017). If they didn't try to sell their products to the sick, only those who suffer from illness would purchase the product based on a genuine demand, not the idea that was created into our minds through mental programming. A millionaire's investment is a good one for as long as there are willing employees to help keep the business going.

The advertisements do not mention that among the adverse effects that aren't always mentioned in the label include depression, loss of appetite or rage, psychosis suicidal ideas, tics, seizures, blood circulation issues or sudden death, depression, and even addiction to drugs that is more troubling considering that the majority of cases stem from a misdiagnosis, as that of gifted kids , and in the instance of Lindsay Lohan, (Woliver, 2010).).

I constantly warn my children about the dangers of substances. If they are addicted to them the chemistry that is in the body will alter, and they'll change into an entirely different person. I want my children to be who they are. I love them exactly as they are. They sometimes have a temper However, so did I when I was my age. They're full of energy and it does not bother me. I'd rather instruct them to shut down often when I need to sleep, rather than putting them to bed so that I can feel at ease.

They are in awe of their ideas and abilities. But if they do ever consume drugs, no matter when they do take controlled drugs such as amphetamines or placebos in any shape or form, they'll lose their grasp of reality and the real world along with all of the consequences that result from it. They will be taught to rely on something to appear "normal" just like Dumbo "depended" on the feather to fly. Maybe the medication will encourage kids to relax and still, or maybe they'll be able to enjoy the drug but we have to consider what's most essential, in order to keep the school as well as the teachers and even the people watching or to combat the wrong assumptions.

The opinion of parents

I read the comments of people from all over the world under ADHD posts. I am interested in learning what people's opinions are about ADHD as well as of the medication. I've had many occasions to hear opinions about ADHD across the world via my social media groups. One group had 78,456 members , while another was 11.379 at the time of June of 2018. However, both are growing rapidly every day and especially the first. I won't discuss their names however you could join any support group on social networks for parents of "ADHD kids," and you'll notice that the posts are routine and are insistently promoting medication, to the point of battling any person who is opposed to.

I've noticed several trends. The posts are always about the angry eruptions of their children that are taking medication, their distraction as well as about the discrimination. They frequently discuss hyperactivity, IEP (Individualized Educational Plans) or the 504 (plan to support students who have disabilities). They all support one another and, in the majority of cases, with respect but if they're off-putting, they are kicked off the team. Whatever the subject or the topic, in one way or another discussions often return to the topic of medication.

I am truly amazed by how casually they discuss different types of medicines and the side consequences. One of the guidelines of these groups is that we cannot ever try to convince parents not to prescribe medication or administer medication to their child, since it is an "personal" choice. However, this does not mean that the child has made the decision to take medication on their own as majority of the time, they aren't inclined to do so and are always in conflict with their parents, because they are openly against. I've seen the questions a lot: "How do I get my son/daughter to take his/her medication?" A lot of parents hide it in their drinks or even in their food items.

Parents of these groups are able to defend ADHD with great passion. If someone tries to make comments against ADHD like, "it is an invented condition" One will be met with comments such as "Ignorant," "educate yourself," "I have ADHD," "It is real for me," "tell that to my kid." I've heard many instances of these types of comments and so will you by joining the online ADHD help group. Parents tend to be extremely passionate about it. Commercials like those mentioned in the previous paragraph actually are effective.

The comments I recently read was different from all the others. The video shows an intelligent boy who is spending the entire day at school and is completely irritated over his homework. His mother writes on her blog:

(sic) "It's thirty minutes since I started trying to convince him to read three paragraphs... I'm at the end my rope. It's week two of school, and my first day of work."

The child is trying to communicate with her about what he wants, and she isn't able to comprehend the message. She's not listening to his pleas, and she doesn't allow him to play like a kid and relax the way he ought to as he has to complete his homework to ensure the success of his grades as well as his future.

I have a connection to this mother. If someone is being influenced by the traditional educational system the person can become annoyed by this method. It is what happened to my wife and me. When that occurred, I was aware of how little I knew that I could have was doing the same thing as my mother did. I used to pressure my children to do things that would make them feel bad for their behavior, but no longer. Nowadays, I am more on their perspective, and look at things from their point of view. Sometimes, this means fighting with the school and teachers however for the good of my children I am open to that kind of new challenge. I am aware that not many people are of my view, and in reality they believe that ADHD is an illness of the brain or mental that requires medical attention.

Random Posts

In the next subsection, I'll provide some of the comments I received from some of my ADHD group on the internet. As always I will not reveal the names of parents who make comments.

Try to decipher the meaning behind the words. Try to guess what they are thinking about their kids as well as about ADHD. Try to deduce the situation. Try to imagine the emotions of the person and then think about what they're thinking. Determine if they're biased or if they are acting according to their expertise. If we're careful and attentive, we can gain much through their words.

Commentaries like these appear on a regular on a regular basis within my ADHD Support groups online. (The comments are written exactly as they appeared in my social networks. I did not correct the mistakes made by the parent.)

On Medication:

1. "Both of my boys have taken Vyvanse but were having anger issues while taking it so we are going to try Concerta."

2. "I require assistance. My son has had Adderall and Vyvanse, and we return on Thursday to try another one. What are you doing which hasn't impacted them badly?"

3. "Does any of your children use dyanavel? My daughter will begin this week. Is it a good or bad thing? Thanks."

4. "Im just starting the process for my daughter, she is 5 and has ADHD/ODD takes 10mg addrerall."

5. "Yes. It takes a while for the body to to react to the medication after a time. The majority of mine experience headaches (and may feel a bit anxious) in the initial days while her body is adjusted. Be sure to drink plenty of fluids as well. Best of luck. Our experience is well worth the adjustment phase."

6. "My daughter was first treated by biphentin. Then she was treated with Vyvanse.

I was then listening to an audiobook that a friend's psychiatrist recommended to her called Driven to Distraction . I thought ...."OMG! I am ADD too! That's why I went through the various hoops my doctor suggested I undergo, in order to treat myself."

7. "After we started putting my son on meds , I began taking them as well! I've known for a long time that I had ADHD also, but no tests were ever done!"

8. "I assure you, mother that it's okay to take medication. Take a shot. You're not in the wrong with your child. You're not taking an easiest route out. You want for your kid to have the greatest chance to succeed. Keep going" !"

9. "Medicine isn't the end all the world, however, it not the very effective by itself. Studies show that it works most effective when it is paired with treatment for behavior modification."

10. "The first time I handed my daughter, age 8, Ritalin(5mg) I broke down in tears.

My husband called me to work, and he unloaded the medication for 2 hours. At times, I couldn't even understand him, I was sobbing."

11. "Clonidine 10mg at night to help her relax and get off to sleep."

12. "Have you Heard of Vayarin? A psychiatrist recommended that we test it and we didn't notice any positive effects until after three months. My daughter, in fact, was extremely emotional and aggressive."

13. "I also felt that the same way. My doctors were pushing me, as did his teachers. I felt as if I was forced to choose. However, he's SO more comfortable with the subject."

14. "This medication is great for beginning, but you'll need more and more attention. Avoid this medication even if you're not sure if you suffer from ADHD or hypertension."

15. "Need assistance .... Teacher of our son called me and informed me that my

son had been quite disrespectful during class today , and later that night it was when he played with an lighter. We started with 1 mg, and it worked fantastically, but the effect ended after 2 months and we decided to increase the dose. Then it appears to have come back to normal and the aggression has begun. I'm aware that this has occurred to many others. Do we increase or switch to a different medication?"

16. "He finally did something that made me feel like I had no choice but to medicate cuz if the behavior continued he would wind up in jail."

17. My kid off his meds........NO!!!!!!! Omg. He's extremely loud. He is everywhere!

What do you think you noticed? Let me explain what I've noticed. I see a lot of insecurity, as well as a ignorance. However, I am amazed that despite that they keep on medicating their children. The social Construct I talked about at the start in this article is now clearly illustrated. Doctors and schools push parents to take their medication. Parents worry that their children are criminals if they aren't taking medication. Parents are convinced that their children are suffering from a disease. Parents aren't sure about the need for medication, however when they do decide to take medicine they look for ways to calm their conscience. Parents tend to lean towards the side of research in medical science, research and medicine, instead of using common wisdom. Parents blame their children, however, they overlook the fact that the educational system is outdated. Parents don't realize the fact that the "ADHD" kids, as they refer to them, aren't sick. Parents are heavily dependent on medication. These are just some of the things I observe in my posts on a regular basis.

It's irrational to think that children have a medical condition and require treatment for a condition which is difficult to identify objectively. It's not just children who have obvious brain damage nowadays, but children who are distracted due to any reason, it could be the inability for learning, stress or just plain boredom. These side effects don't have any significance, as long as medications simulate the characteristics of a "normal" kid, as in the old school guidelines.

Medication Side Effects

Medical advances have certainly helped save lives. But, the majority of medications need to be taken with care since they may cause adverse consequences, and some of them could kill us. We should suppose that someone is taking medication because they are suffering from a condition more severe than the side effect. There is no reason to take medication when being healthy and feeling well only to experience uncomfortable adverse consequences. I can understand the use of cancer medications as well as for MS and for certain classes of diabetes, the flu and other ailments which are extremely unpleasant and can be detected by testing for blood or any other examinations that are objective. But in the case of ADHD I'm not so sure to take medication, since the majority of these children are healthy.

I will explain to readers potential side effects found in the labeling for ADHD medication. These consequences can be "possible" but they actually are commonplace, as evident from the comments I've read on blog posts from parents in actual situations. The information I've provided can be found by typing, as an example, "Vayarin side effects," using any web browser. If you type this in you will be presented with an extensive list of adverse reactions, however, for each medication I will only mention five of the ones I picked randomly. These are the exact names of brands that I that I have mentioned in my previous posts.

Vayarin

1. Bleeding gums

2. Dizziness

3. Unusual heartbeat

4. Paralysis

5. The coughing up of blood

Clonidine

1. Severe chest pain

2. A severe headache

3. Anxiety

4. Tired or irritable

5. Insomnia

Ritalin (Metilphenidate)

1. Nausea and vomiting

2. Problems with vision

3. Numbness

4. Psychosis

5. Palpitations

Concerta

1. Nausea and vomiting

2. Problems with vision

3. Numbness

4. Psychosis

5. Palpitations

Biphentin (Methylphenidate)

1. Anxiety, nervousness, or agitation

2. Dizziness

3. Stomach pain

4. Trouble sleeping

5. Palpitations

Vyanese

1. Feeling irritable or hyper.

2. Poor appetite

3. Poor circulation

4. Vision Changes

5. Racing heartbeat

Adderall (Amphetamine)

1. Nervousness

2. Excitability

3. A loss of appetite

4. Hair loss

5. Vomiting

Dyanavel

1. Stomach pain

2. Inability to eat

3. Nosebleeds

4. Headache

5. Changes in mood

Personally the mere fact of being aware of these adverse consequences is reason enough for me to not take medication for children. As I mentioned I would do it should if I could tell that their lives was at risk however, it's not. Parents often ask themselves the reason why their children are depressed, moody, or losing weight, or why they're stressed, or even insane. The solution is quite simple. Read the label on the medication you're giving them. You're concerned about what the school will say regarding what the future holds for your kids However, you're not thinking about their present.

The withdrawal and addiction effects are something that isn't discussed as a possible result, but it's a real thing like it is for person trying to eliminate the effects of drugs out of their body. Certain of these drugs include Adderall could be addictive substances (RxList).

In the TED speech of Neurobiologist David Anderson (2013) He explains that the brain isn't just the same as a chemical soup containing serotonin, norepinephrine, and dopamine and that drugs claim to treat complex mental disorders as if it could be able to differentiate between all the chemical components within the brain. Anderson says that the drugs are a plethora of adverse effects, and treating the symptoms of a complex disorder like schizophrenia is similar to making a change to your car's oil by opening the can and pouring it on the block of your car. A few drops will flow into the correct place but the majority of it can cause much more harm than good."

In the first chapter, I argued that the concept of ADHD has been marketed to us. It's time to think whether this is true. I believe in what I am saying since I have been aware of the society around me by the huge number of students I have and hundreds of families who are in my support groups as well as by watching my children as well as the education system, and by looking at the materials I've devoted myself to. If you're not certain of what I am saying look for the answers. If you make a mistake, like I claim it to be it's a large mistake that has a huge impact for our children and our future generations.

Chapter 16: Some Top Tips For Getting Organized And Controlling Clutter

The most prominent characteristics of ADHD include inattention as well as the ability to be distracted, making business one of the biggest challenges grown-ups with the disorder must face. If you suffer from ADHD the thought of being organized, be you're at your workplace or home, may cause you to feel overwhelmed.

You can also figure ways to break down tasks into smaller, smaller steps, and implement a structured method to run your business. Through implementing various regimens and frameworks, as well as benefiting from tools like day-to-day planners and ideas, you will be able to ensure that you are in control and also manage the chaos.

Set up a framework and cool behavioursand ensure they stay up

To arrange your space office, home, or even a workplace Begin by categorizing your possessions, and deciding on what is essential and which are able to be recycled or saved. To organize yourself, get into your habit of keeping your mind checklists and making lists. Make sure to keep your newly organized plan in the context of your daily routines.

Create space. Find out what you need every day and find storage containers or wardrobes to store things you do not. Mark specific areas to keep things like expenses, secrets and other things that are easily misplaced. Get rid of things you don't need.

Utilize a calendar app or a day planner. Making the use of a day planner or an app for your smartphone or computer will help you organize your dates and appointments. It can also help you remember your target dates. By using digital calendars you could create automatic reminders so that you don't forget scheduled events. off your radar.

Use checklists. Make use of lists and notes to keep track at a regular basis for scheduled job, deadlines, tasks as well as visits. If you choose to utilize a day-to-day coordinator, be sure to keep all lists and notes in it. There are a lot of options to use your smartphone or computer system. Find "to do" apps or task managers.

Do the issue now.You will avoid the loss of memory, clutter as well as lazyness by organizing documents, cleaning up mess, or returning a your call promptly but not in the near future. If the task is completed within 2 minutes or lesser, then do immediately instead of saving it for later.

Keep your paper trail clean

If you suffer from the disorder of attention (ADHD) previously called ADD everything you do, from keeping your bills on time to keeping on top of your work and household obligations, as well as social demands can be frustrating. ADHD presents challenges to adults from all walks of their lives. It could be detrimental to your health and your professional and personal collaborations. Your symptoms could lead to excessive procrastination, difficulties keeping track of deadlines, as well as spontaneous actions. In addition, you might believe that family members and friends don't know what you're going through.

If you suffer from ADHD and you are a chronically stressed person, paperwork may be an important part of your disorganization. However, you can put an end to the endless piles of documents and letters scattered across your kitchen and workdesks, or this. All you need is time to create a paper system that will benefit you. Manage mail every day. You should set aside a few minutes every day to sort through the mail, usually when you receive it. It is helpful to have an area where you can organize your mail, and then either throw it away, send it or take action on it.

Go paperless. Reduce your paper to keep track of. Demand digital statements and expense reports instead of paper copies. If you live in the U.S., you can cut down on spam by abstaining from the Direct Marketing Association's (DMA) Mail Choice Solution.

Create a ling system. Utilize dividers or separate document folders to store different kinds of documents (such as medical records, invoices and even financial statements). Label and color code your documents to ensure that you have the information you require quickly.

Tips to manage your time and keeping to your the schedule

Time monitoring is an atypical symptom of ADHD. It is possible to lose your track of time, forget deadlines and squirm, not knowing the amount of time you require to complete your tasks, or find yourself performing tasks in the incorrect sequence. Many adults with ADHD spend their time working on one thing - referred to by the term "hyper-focusing"-- that virtually nothing else gets accomplished. This can cause you to be with a sense of frustration and incompetence and cause others to be agitated. But, there are ways to help you handle your time.

Time management tips

Adults suffering from Attention De Cit disorder typically suffer from a divergent perception of the exact way in which time moves. To ensure that you have a consistent view of time with that of anyone other than you, try the first method in the book that is A clock.

Make yourself an avid clock-watcher. Utilize a watch or a prominent wall or desk clock to help you keep track of the time. If you start a project write down the time by either stating it in a loud voice or writing the time down.

Utilize timers.Allocate your self a set amount of time for each task and set up an alarm or timer to inform you when your time is over. If you have a longer task, think about setting up an alarm that goes every few minutes to ensure you are aware and aware of how long time is being wasted.

You should give your self more time than you'll need. Adults suffering from ADHD are notoriously bad when it comes to estimating how long it takes to complete a task. For every half hour of time you believe it will take to go somewhere or finish the job, offer your own an additional padding by adding 10 minutes..

Be early and schedule reminders. Note consultations up to 15 minutes before they actually are. Set up a plan to get home on time, and ensure that you've got everything you require before leaving, so you're not trying to locate your phone or keys once you're ready to leave.

Tips for prioritizing

As adults who suffer from ADHD typically struggle with the issue of impulse control as and can jump between one task and another based on task, nishing tasks can be difficult and large tasks can be to be a bit difficult. To combat this,

Determine what tasks you will tackle first. Find out what the most important tasks that you must accomplish then set your other priorities after one.

Begin by taking things one at one time.Break smaller jobs or divide them into smaller, more manageable steps. Be on track. Be sure not to get distracted by sticking to your plan by using a timer. You can apply it, if needed.

Learn to say no

The urge to be impulsive can cause adults with ADHD to sign up for multiple tasks at work or engage in numerous social connections. However, a busy schedule can make you feel confused or exhausted and negatively impact the performance of the work you do. By avoiding specific commitments could boost your ability to finish tasks, stay on top of social schedules and live an active lifestyle. Examine your daily routine before allowing something completely new.

Chapter 17: Determine The Problem

It is often overwhelming to look at the many issues your ADHD can cause for you and to envision ways to conquer these issues, and be able to live your life in an efficient and organized way.There are solutions you can devise to deal with this, but first , you have to cut down each piece of the issues that hinder your way of achieving what has to be done, not just every day, but on a minute by minutes basis.

It doesn't mean that you must track the entirety of your time individually.But for a day, try to take a break each time you're confronted with a problem and record what it is.Start at the moment you wake up as well as the morning routine.How do you prepare yourself for the next day? Is there anything that hinders you from carrying even the most basic tasks? These are the kinds of things distract you and make you late for work, school or wherever you're required to go next.It could be like not being able to locate something you'll need to prepare yourselflike a toothbrush, trousers, one shoe or anything else.

Don't be afraid to talk about the things.Be aware that they could be the things you've encountered throughout your life, and could trigger anxieties for you to talk about them regardless of whether the sheet you write them down on is for your own use and to assist yourself.Do not let your feelings of anxiety hinder you.If your experience symptoms like this, you should you should take a break, lay downand take a deep breath.

Be aware that you are not focusing on these issues to make yourself look bad or to dwell on your past failures.You are doing this so that the next day will have the same hardships.You have been accused previously of being an avid daydreamer.People think that it means that you are not focused. focus.Prove that they, as well as the inner voice that nags at you, wrong. make use of your daydreaming to imagine your ideal life where you are able to get dressed each day without delays because of misplacing basic items.Imagine what you'll do to incorporate the systems in your daily routine that keep it in the order in your life and allow you to keep your commitments as well as your concentration.Then once you have this new lifestyle clearly in your head Take a deep breath, and then return on your list.Write down the things you did not identify that stopped you from sticking to the schedule.And continue to your day.If this happens again , you can use the same strategies to bring your attention back to the right track.

If you are unable to locate an item of clothing or a product you wear to dress yourself There is the preemptive solution to that.To "preempt" something means to take action to stop an event that is anticipated from happening.This is the reason we first must determine what the anticipated situation is.Then we are able to come up with an option to stop it from occurring.

You'll be going through your day and document all obstacles to in line with the schedule.How do you know if something can be considered one of these obstructions? What is the best way to define a responsible and productive person? A person who can have satisfying career and relationships? The person who is punctual to appointments and commitments.So should something be making you late, it will be onto your list.That person is relaxed and focused.So when something is making you be stressed or stressed or in some way it will be on the list.If something is making you to feel exhausted and disorganized or in some way it is to the top of the list.

Prompting and Systems

You've been sincere, honest and not judging the issues you face throughout the day.You have an outline of all your issues before you.Read it over.Now as you work through the next few days, whenever you spot any of these issues it should appear as the "prompt" to you.You can take this prompt as a signal to know that this is the moment you need to put into action the strategy you'll develop to overcome the issue.

What is a "system"? A system is a planned and method of organization that allows you to deal with the issues that prevent you from successfully getting things done and keeping track of things.They are strategies that you come up with to help you.These strategies are best implemented and executed when you have the appropriate tools to aid you.

Tools

The first tool we will use is a calendar that starts at the moment we get up each day.Adults who suffer from ADHD are more likely to hit the sleep button on their alarm clock or oversleep as their attention is focused upon what they need at the moment, not on what they'll need over the long run.No no more snooze! Sorry! This is an entirely new set of rules you'll establish of doing what you need to do right now and not postponing things off.This begins with sleep.It may sound a bit gruelling, sure.But it will be an integral part of your routine and you'll be able to thank you for your discipline that you demonstrated when you first started, prior to waking up when your first alarm was a routine.

The next step in your agenda is to plan out your schedule, giving a predetermined time for every part of getting prepared needs.This must be as specific like brushing your teeth washing your hair the time you will choose your outfit, and so on.

To make this be effective, the next instrument you should be equipped with organization.Have you heard the phrase, "A place for everything with everything put in it's place?"Well take a moment to get used to hearing it because it's the new mantra.When you take off your clothes in the evening, they are put straight back onto the hanger, if they're not dirty enough or go into the hamper in case they're soiled.You do not need an area in your bedroom or in a pile to put your clothes and then pick the clothes out of.Invest in some new and stylish hangers that you will love with your garments to put them on.This is a reward you can give yourself.We tend to throw things away in the areas we love the ones we've set aside to store them in.Spend some time organizing your drawers and revel at how it appears once you have worked it out.Take your time during your time to put up the shoe rack, or store your shoes in boxes.

Pinterest can be described as a social network site where people regularly discuss ideas to help with organization.Look to it as a challenge that you can take on.It is difficult and unfamiliar to you, and this will bring your attention to the task at hand and focus your attention on the work of organizing.And the good news is that once you have mastered it and stop focusing on the general task of organizing it is not necessary to be actively organizing anymore.You simply must keep the routine of throwing everything away when it is gone or is no longer of immediate use for you.This will be done due to your own prompts, since if you are stuck because you've lost track of your things, you'll return to your system.You must ensure that the process of organizing and organizing your stuff so enjoyable for you as possible.By making sure you are proud of the way you organize, it will keep your straight and on track.That physical clutter that is in front of you is transformed into confusion and chaos in your head.

Another time-waster that is frequently reported is the baffling event losing your keys.When you enter the home, the keys have to have a spot to go.No Ifs, or ands or ifs about it.You have to be strict with yourself.Every when you come into the home, put your keys into this newly created space.Buy yourself a charming hook and place it close to the front door. You can also take a dish that you like and put it on the table near your door.Again make sure that the experience is as pleasant and enjoyable as it can.These are all parts of your systems.And be aware that these systems were created by and are implemented according to your prompts.For instance, if you realize that you're getting behind because you've lost a shoe , or keys, it's an opportunity to return in your routine.

We must remain optimistic about ourselves and be willing to share our successes with others around us so that they can encourage us.They ought to be encouraged to inquire about how you're doing in your system and routines.It is crucial for people who suffer from ADHD to take responsibility for the people who are close to them.After all, no one wants to disappoint their loved ones.So make time to inform those who you cherish about the work you're doing.When they notice that you're getting better, you'll have a enthusiastic, highly efficient cheerleading squad.This could be the most important thing.

However, if you are finding that this is not happening, do not be ashamed to sit down with them again and let them know how important it is for your success to receive these words of inspiration.Sometimes people are just so wrapped up in their busy lives that they will notice your advancements, but only comment in their head.Perhaps they are embarrassed to share these thoughts with you.Let them know you need them and they will be happy to oblige.This will make your closest personal relationships infinitely more rewarding.And do not forget to mention to them when you notice positive things about them! This can also boost confidence in yourself because we all want to feel like we are a component of someone's happiness.

It is important to be patient and take things slowly.Do not attempt to rush to fix the problem within a single day or the span of a week.Be gentle with yourself.You might have heard of the phrase "baby steps," or even "one step at a time." It is your time to create the new habits and systems.It might not seem like it when you're in crisis or panic situation, but you do.This is not a reason to put everything off.This procedure takes a every day effort.When you can see how much you are able to do, you'll be motivated to accomplish more and more every day.You will also cultivate satisfaction when you are in areas that you have previously struggled.However it is important to remember that if you're someone who is driven by deadlines like we mentioned earlier set yourself an exact date and communicate the deadline with someone in your life whom you would not like to disappoint.Ask them to not only hold your hand to the deadline however, they should also be encouraging you and congratulate you for your accomplishments.

We must continue to create lists.The foremost list you've got should be that of your "to-do list." Buy an organized notebook and keep a daily list of all the things you need to do.Any small thing you have to complete should be placed onto the list.And what is most crucial to remember is to mark each task off when it's accomplished.You should feel proud of yourself when you complete the tasks done.You will reward yourself for every task accomplished.If this means that you allow yourself a bit more time for yourself, or when this is the case, you can buy yourself a treat, or whatever it is for you, set the reward and offer yourself regular reward.We will be able to get more rewards in the future.

Review Your "to-do list" throughout the day, but you should start the evening by taking a seat and writing down everything you will need to complete the next day.Research has proven that getting organized prior to bed can help get your head in order and help to put your mind to rest easier.The following day, once you've got yourself prepared and gotten yourself ready, review the "to-do list" and make another list that is shorter of the things that is to be accomplished in that day.Not all of the items that is on the "to-do list" will be accomplished this day.When you have completed items from your list during the duration of the day, make sure you take that smaller to check it out at night. You can then check those items off again.Seeing the tasks get crossed off twice will help you feel proud of how successful you've been.Be satisfied with your accomplishments and be sure to reward yourself.

Do your best to finish the task at the time you are able to complete them, and when that's not feasible, then mark them off your "to-do list".Especially in the event that the task is complex and long begin immediately and take on the toughest parts of the job you'd usually delay first.Do not think to yourself that you will have enough time to tackle it later.If you start contemplating these thoughts take a break, get your mind off of it, refocus and finish the task immediately.

Patterns, Rewards, and Habits

As these systems become ingrained in your routine they become "patterns." A pattern is a regular and intelligible form or sequence discernible in certain action or situations.Developing these systems into patterns occurs within the inner workings of your brain through repetition.Soon you will be coming home and dropping your keys in their designated spot without even thinking about it.Your clothes will come off and be hung up as a matter of routine.You know that doing so will get you what you need, which is to be responsible and on time and it will just get it done.When you notice that this is something you are accomplishing, that's time to give yourself a "reward."

We are certain that you've heard of reward in the past, we want to make sure that we define it as something that is that is given to acknowledge one's efforts, service or achievement.It is in sync with the huge efforts that you're putting into this process.So be sure to give yourself a reward even before you can see the results of your work to ensure that you are able to enjoy the fruits.The results of your efforts will depend on how well you're getting over the way your ADHD holds your back.This is obviously a kind of reward in and of its own, and it could be considered the most gratifying reward.But we're talking about smaller rewards.Is there anything you refuse yourself for fear of telling yourself that you are unable to afford it? Now is the perfect time to offer it to yourself.Because when you achieve the goals laid out here and achieving them, you will be able to succeed in your work and we hope, that money will be less of a concern in the future for you.Giving yourself a small bite of cake to thank yourself for a successful week of a healthy diet is an excellent reward.Letting yourself enjoy the show you love to satisfy your desire for "guilty pleasure"--that's an incentive reward.The benefits will be greater than any fears you may feel about the indulgence.And the rewards should be distributed in the smallest amounts of completion of tasks, especially when you've broken tasks into segments since that's something that you struggle to keep.

The reason is that the rewards assist in developing routines, systems as well as patterns that turn into "habits." This is an outcome of new research which is discussed in media across the world.We develop habits by following the instructions, the routine and then the following by rewarding ourselves with a reward.Then we've got the term habit.A routine is a stable or routinely-occurring habit or practice, particularly one that is difficult to abandon up.We are focusing on the two elements of this definition that are crucial to us.First We have been referring to many elements of ADHD that keep you from success to tendencies.With this new approach, you'll be developing new habits that will lead to success.Doesn't that make you happy?

As the new systems develop into habits in the brain, and you are rewarded, it will be difficult to give these rewards up.Why should you even want to do that if you're not only watching but experiencing the accomplishments you have achieved? However, we also don't want to let go of the rewards we enjoy! These new habits will allow you to maintain healthy, satisfying jobs and relationships that believed were beyond your reach.

Conclusion

ADHD is among the conditions that children can develop therefore you shouldn't be worried about it. Find out and seek medical attention for your child since the earlier you start the better it will be for your child and your whole family.

Furthermore while it is true that it demands lots of things when dealing with children with ADHD but it doesn't mean that your child can't succeed in school. All it takes is persistence, patience, and co-operation with the child's providers, and all is well.

Parents of children who suffer from ADHD should also be aware that they should be involved in their children's daily to routine activities, as some children tend to leave a lot of it to their caregivers and medical professionals. Participation in activities lets the child feel that you're with them throughout the whole process and that you are there for them. Your care and love will benefit children in ways that you could never imagine.

www.ingramcontent.com/pod-product-compliance
Lightning Source LLC
Chambersburg PA
CBHW060332030426
42336CB00011B/1312